Organize Your Day:

17 Easy Strategies to Manage Your Day, Improve Productivity & Overcome Procrastination

3rd Edition

Dane Taylor

not engaging in the rendering of legal, financial, medical or professional advice.

By reading this document, the reader agrees that under no circumstances are we responsible for any losses, direct or indirect, which are incurred as a result of the use of information contained within this document, including, but not limited to, —errors, omissions, or inaccuracies.

Table of Contents

Introduction

This book contains proven steps and strategies on how to manage your daily schedule more effectively, be more productive, and as a result achieve more in life while also reducing the clutter and stress around you. It will help you achieve the levels of success and happiness in your life that you desire, while overcoming procrastination and disorganization – remember that these are two major things that kill success! It's time to put an end to that now.

The goal of this book is to be a breath of fresh air and also an inspiration for you – if you think that being organized on a daily basis requires lots of time-consuming planning and a strict personality, you're WRONG! It's much easier than that. Anybody CAN take control of their life and organize their day without being a strictly detail-oriented person. The key to getting things done is simply this: building effective daily habits that become a normal, natural routine for you.

This book is going to teach you how to get started doing just that. You see, anybody can just spell out a list of time management techniques that you should follow. But what I've seen in most people is a DISCONNECT between learning the techniques and actually IMPLEMENTING them consistently in their lives. This is where most people fail, so I'm going to teach you how to avoid this and become the most productive version of yourself possible! And of course, there are 17 core productivity and time management techniques you'll learn throughout reading this book. I consider these techniques to be the most essential, game-changing things you can do to improve your organization, productivity, and get things done in life. Without further ado, let's get started. Here's to your success!

P.S. Make sure you read through the whole book, as there's a special bonus gift waiting for you at the end! Happy reading!

Chapter 1: Getting the Right Mindset and Killing the Source of Procrastination!

Before going into all the specific time management techniques to help you become more organized every day, we first need to lay a solid foundation for you to stay motivated *every day* and nip procrastination in the bud. Like I mentioned earlier, you could learn all the time management techniques in the world – but if you struggle with procrastination, it will stop you dead in your tracks. It's impossible to achieve your goals if you perpetually put off working on them until tomorrow, especially when tomorrow never comes!

Many people have absolutely no problem admitting that they have a procrastination problem, but relatively few understand what procrastination is. There are plenty of jokes and funny quotes that make light of procrastination, but the truth is that the "I'll get to that someday" mentality is a serious issue that's standing between you and your dreams of success.

Let's start by shedding some light on this seldom discussed topic. Understanding what procrastination is is the very first step in overcoming it – and once you are ready to stop waiting for "someday" to come, your journey to a more organized, productive life can truly begin.

What is procrastination, and why is it a problem?

Procrastination is not a problem with time management, nor do procrastinators have issues with planning. They know what they should be doing and when – they just have a problem getting started. Put simply, procrastination is the art of putting off. Procrastinators are not selective – they'll put anything off, whether it's work related, family related or life related. And if you are going to organize your day, you need to find a way to overcome procrastination.

The thing to remember is that procrastinators are made, not born. There's no physical or genetic trait that makes someone prone to postponing completing necessary tasks. This is great news: it means you can do something about it! Procrastination is a learned behavior, and it can be unlearned.

In the same way, organization is a learned behavior, so what you need to do is to replace the 'bad' learned behavior – procrastination – with 'good' learned behavior – organization. It's simply a matter of replacing a pattern of habits that don't work for you with new patterns that are designed to make you happier and more successful.

Getting rid of procrastination is an absolute necessity. It's the one thing in your life you absolutely can't wait to do. If you try, you'll discover that all you're doing is storing up future stress for yourself. All those tasks you've been putting off can't go undone forever, and this may have negative effects on all aspects of your life – work, family, relationships, and even your health itself. Procrastination can cause serious financial troubles, increase your stress and anxiety levels, and even contribute to chronic insomnia and other sleep problems. If you've ever spent a sleepless night thinking about all of the things you know you should be doing, procrastination has already had a negative impact on your life!

There's an old saying that 'Procrastination is the thief of time.' If you are a procrastinator, you are stealing time from yourself – time that could be so much more productive if you could only kick the procrastination habit. Not only are you losing precious time to procrastination, you're losing happiness. When you stop procrastinating, you stop needing to worry about all the things that have to be done – and that gives you back the ability to actually enjoy your life!

Why do I procrastinate?

There are four main reasons for procrastination. They all have one thing in common: they're emotional, rather than physical reasons. This is great news, because emotional problems can be addressed through diligent, consistent effort. You'll find specific techniques to address procrastination later in this chapter, but at this point, what you want to do is identify what's causing you to put off doing the things you know need to be done. Once you do that, and have identified, your own particular reason – or combination of reasons – you're well on the way to dealing with your procrastination problem.

Procrastination Cause #1: The fear of failure

Some people procrastinate because they fear they will fail. This is possibly the most understandable of the reasons. Every undertaking comes with risks: no one is successful at everything, every time.

Think about how you approach various tasks and initiatives. Some people look at every challenge and can only see positive outcomes, while others have a clear vision of impending catastrophe. If you are one of those people who think about all the potentials for disaster in the undertaking, and imagine all the different things that may go wrong in your enterprises, the fear of failure is probably contributing to your procrastination issue.

You probably don't subscribe to the 'I didn't fail, I just found lots of ways that didn't work' mindset. You probably believe it's better to avoid doing anything that could go wrong. If you don't do anything, nothing can go wrong. This sounds like a sensible approach, but it is going to keep you from being successful. Pretty much anything that is worth your attention also has the unfortunate potential for disaster. In fact, the more complex and ultimately rewarding the project happens to be, the more openings for error there are likely to be. It's just the way it is.

People who fear failure also tend to worry about their friends and family. What will these people think of you if your best efforts turn out not to be good enough? They wonder how those closest to them might react to their failure, even if they are usually very supportive. Many times, people who procrastinate envision the people they know mocking, scorning, or even being angry at them for trying something new. If any of this sounds like you, the fear of failure could be what's causing your procrastination problem.

Procrastination Cause #2: The fear of succeeding!

Some people are scared of failing, and others are scared of succeeding. That might not sound rational, yet it happens frequently. Even the most ambitious people can be affected in this way. There are times when you want to achieve something so much it physically hurts, and when that happens, you will find all sorts of reasons why things won't work out as you want them to.

The fear of success is really the fear that you won't be able to handleyou're your life will change if you are successful. Let's look at your goal of becoming more organized and productive. This sounds like a fantastic goal: what could possibly be the downside of achieving it? But our minds are funny things, capable of generating entire litanies of things to worry about.

Perhaps you find yourself believing that, even while you strive to be the best you possibly can at your job, if you are too good, maybe your boss, your colleagues and everyone who knows you is going to expect even more from you, and you won't be able to deliver. Then you could find yourself worrying how on earth you will manage to top your personal best performance, and continue to improve consistently. You may feel there is only so much one person can achieve, but that's just not true. Your fear may be limiting you, but in fact you have the potential to accomplish anything and everything you set out to do. All you need is the right mindset.

Another problem arises when you believe that if you become too successful, even more responsibilities will fall on you. Struggling with balancing our work lives and our personal lives is a challenge for everyone. If you show you're capable of doing more, will you be given so much more to do that you'll no longer be able to maintain your work/life balance in the way you want to? Maybe you fear success will intrude too deeply into your personal life, and other people will learn more about the real you behind the professional persona. Not everyone is able to cope with that.

If any of this sounds familiar to you, fear of success may be contributing to your problems with procrastination.

Procrastination Cause #3: You are a perfectionist

There is an old adage that goes like this: 'If a job is worth doing at all, then it's worth doing well.' Like most old sayings, there's more than an element of truth in it. The trouble is, some people take the wisdom behind the saying to another level. Doing something well isn't good enough: if they're going to take on a task, it must be performed absolutely perfectly, to the highest standard. If they can't do that, they will put off even starting the task– often indefinitely.

That can be a sensible strategy in some ways, since putting a little distance between yourself and a project that's causing you headaches will mean you can return to it later with some fresh ideas and renewed motivation. The problems start when 'later' never comes. The perfect can absolutely be the enemy of the good, especially when longing for the ultimate outcome means you wind up with no outcome at all!

That's procrastination, and it's probably because you're a

perfectionist. If that's the case, maybe you should learn train yourself to set your expectations of yourself at a more realistic and achievable level.

Procrastination Cause #4: You grew up in an authoritarian environment as a child

As has been mentioned, procrastination is learned behavior that is often an instinctive response to early life experiences. You might have been born American, English or whatever, but one thing is certain - you were not born a procrastinator. That came about because at some stage, you rebelled against strictures you could do nothing about. Procrastination is your way of fighting back.

Perhaps your Mom or Dad was strict when you were a kid. You either could not or would not defy them openly, so you became a procrastinator as a kind of defense mechanism. Alongside this, your self-development in the planning and organizing area would have suffered because you grew up in the background of an authoritarian home environment.

When you grow up in a home which is highly regulated and controlled, when you are instructed what to do and when you should do it, you will inevitably miss out on one of life's vital skills. You don't get the chance to learn how to formulate and adhere to schedules, or how to produce a workable 'to do' list to ensure that everything gets done at the right time so the project comes together as it should.

As a result of such a strict upbringing, it's likely that you rely on friends rather than your family for support. The problem is, friends can be so much more tolerant of any shortcomings and accept your excuses more readily. Friends probably do not see your procrastination as a real problem, and this can serve to reinforce and perhaps even validate your problem behavior.

While these root causes may be behind your procrastination, sometimes it's just a question of wanting to do something else – anything else! – rather than just getting on with what needs to be done. It could be that if your procrastination habits are deeply ingrained, or if you can't identify the root cause, you may need specialist help. However, assuming that you know what's causing the problem, these strategies can help you overcome procrastination and get on with the business of becoming more organized and successful in life.

Strategies to Conquer Your Procrastination

Make lists

Just about any task you can think of can be converted into a list. And in fact, nothing is more motivational than a list that you can cross things off as you achieve them – provided the list is not so long that it's depressing. Try breaking down various tasks into a number of bite-sized chunks. If you're not sure how to go about this, just think of elements of the task that you can complete in no more than 15 – 30 minutes.

It's preferable for a procrastinator to complete four fifteen minute objectives rather than a single hour-long task. That's because four separate items can be checked off your list, rather than just one. There's a buzz that goes with that achievement which will help to keep you motivated through the remainder of the project.

Talk yourself into it

Don't use words like 'should,' 'must' and 'have to' in conjunction with the project you're putting off. These words have negative connotations. You need to train yourself to think of the task ahead as something you want to do, as opposed to something you have to do.

You must have wanted to undertake the project in the first place, or you wouldn't have committed to it. You need to view the task as something enjoyable that you really want to do, and that means adjusting your internal vocabulary to suit the situation. Choose more positive words to use – convince yourself that you want to do the task, tell yourself you're going to enjoy it – and believe it!

Do something – anything at all!

Often, procrastinators find that getting started on a project is the main problem. If this sounds like you, resolve to do something – anything – to get started on the task. Simply putting a title at the top of a page can be the boost that generates ideas, but even if it doesn't, the title will be fixed in your brain, and that will get you thinking about the task ahead of you. Thinking often leads to action, and before you know it, you're working on the very thing you've been putting off.

If you need to interview specific people for the project, make some calls or send some emails and schedule those interviews. Once they're arranged, you'll need to think about the questions you're going to ask, and the answers you're looking for. That will give your thoughts a specific focus, rather than having them chasing each other around your brain with no real direction.

Visualize the project

Map out the project in your mind, and ask yourself relevant questions. How will you approach each element of the task? What, if any, resources are you going to need? Who do you need to contact for relevant information or advice? Now consider what the finished project will mean to you, and how others may be touched or influenced by it.

Do you need to get important information 'out there?' Is this project going to make life easier for yourself, or for other people? Can you anticipate a period of relaxation when the project is completed? These are all excellent motivators to get working and follow the project through to its conclusion. Visualize the task ahead of you, then go ahead and do it. Now you've played it through in your mind, it's time to put those thoughts into action and get results.

Maybe you have noticed that all the strategies mentioned here are reliant on re-structuring your basic thought patterns, not making adjustments to your schedule. That should convince you that procrastination is a state of mind, not an inability to act. Until you are able to distance yourself from the procrastinating mindset, the success you are aiming for is always going to be something you hope is going to happen 'One Day.' If you are able to overcome procrastination, 'One Day' will arrive much sooner than you ever imagined!

Chapter 2: Identifying Your Why And Overcoming Negativity

The first step to taking control of your life's direction and becoming super productive is to identify a solid Why in your life. Simply put, what is your purpose? One way to think about your purpose is as your primary motivator to get out of bed every day and live your life.

Every single person on this planet is unique. No two people have the same purpose. Some people are what's called intrinsically motivated: they are strongly driven to be the best they can be to satisfy their own perception of themselves. Other people are what's called externally motivated: their purpose comes from having responsibilities, such as the need to take care of their family, or even to live life in accordance with how their faith or culture told them things are meant to be done. Many people have a combination of intrinsic and external motivations in their life, guiding all of their decision making. There's no one right way to be motivated – but it does help tremendously to know what factors are important to you.

Having a strong "Why" will keep you motivated every day to take action and stay on top of things. Living your life in accordance with your purpose feels good. This is because you'll have a goal in sight with a strong reason to achieve it. Your "Why" will be something you can remind yourself of every day when you wake up to motivate yourself and feel like you have a reason to be here on this planet, doing what you do.

It's not as simple as it seems, though. You're going to have to dig deep inside yourself and ask yourself a lot of possibly challenging questions in order to identify your particular Why. It's not just a matter of knowing your goals, although that's a great starting point. You also need to understand why those goals are important to you. When you can understand that, you have your Why.

Your Why should be positive and entirely personal. It is also a very good idea to have your Why be a long term, sustainable thing that is not dependent on other people or events. Remember, in this world, we don't have the ability to control other people's actions, feelings and behaviors. We're only in charge of our own selves. If your purpose is dependent on a factor you have no real influence over – such as making a celebrity fall madly in love with you – you will never be able to be happy.

It's very natural to try to make caring for your loved ones your Why. Just remember, you need to be living your life in order to be able to provide for anyone else. While you may want to succeed because you want to give your family the things you missed out on as a child, the motivation to do so must come from yourself, not from someone else. If it is not your Why, it will not work for you. You need to understand that right from the start, because it's important.

Try this exercise to get you thinking about your personal Why. Take out a piece of paper and a pen and write out your primary goals in life right now. Then write out the strongest reasons why you want to achieve those goals. Here is a simple example to get you started:

Goal: I want to build a business on the side that makes me more money and allows me to quit my job.

Why: I want to have more freedom with my time and finances to enjoy life better and spend more time with family.

Keep working on this, and think of as many goals as you can, large and small. Writing them down as opposed to typing them out will help with the thought processes. And keep thinking about the reasoning and motivations behind those goals. Spend as long as you need to on this.

When you look at your list, you may find that many of your goals have certain motivating traits in common. For example, if your list of goals includes starting the business, getting healthier and traveling more, and the motivation for each includes spending more time with your family, you'll now that the strongest force driving your decisions is your urge to be with your loved ones. This will help you clarify your thought process as you go forward. As you make choices ask yourself, will this give me more time with my family? If the answer is not yes (or even yes, eventually!) then it's not a choice that's in alignment with your authentic life purpose. It's not moving you closer to your Why.

By having some strong reasons like this to motivate you, there will be no stopping you! Once you have your completed list, type it up and print it out, and keep these written statements somewhere you can look over them every morning when you start your day. Identifying your Why is one of the most useful things you can do to set about organizing yourself and becoming more productive. These are some of the reasons why you should identify your Why:

Your Why is a Target

To be more organized, you need to be more focused. Identifying your Why forces you to focus on what you want to achieve, and why those achievements are important to you.

You now have a reason to get out of bed every day, a reason to keep going when things get tough, a reason to push yourself harder when you feel like giving up, and a reason to feel proud of yourself when things work out the way you want them to.

As you work, you will keep your Why foremost in your mind – it will act as a target towards which you are constantly working, in good times and in bad. It will help you to work harder, work longer, and work more efficiently. When things go wrong – which they inevitably will – remember your Why and keep going.

Sometimes life is frustrating. We run into obstacles. Things don't work out the way we want them to. Having your Why helps you maintain your focus so you can stay on track and keep working toward your goals, even when it is hard. It will all be worth it in the end.

Your Why Helps You Believe in Yourself

This world is full of people who have nothing better to do than diminish your dreams. They'll tell you that you're wasting your time, that your goals are impossible, and that you'll never achieve your dreams. Dealing with that kind of doubt is tough – and just to make things even tougher, you might even start to doubt yourself. What if all these negative people are right?

When you know your Why, you have a way to deal with all of this negativity. Let people say what they want to say. You focus on your Why. It will help you believe in yourself and your goals. You can do whatever you want to, because you know exactly why you are doing it. If you need to or want to, you can explain this to others, or you can just hold it in your heart to get you through the doubt.

Your Why helps you to plan and succeed

Knowing exactly why you are doing what you do gives you focus. It helps you to see things more clearly, so that you can work around obstacles, plan for problems, and eventually succeed in business and in life. Think of your plan like a roadmap and your Why as a destination. If you don't care where you're going, you don't need a map. If you don't have a goal in life, any choices will work, since you don't care about the outcome. But when you have a Why – a destination for your life, a place you want to go and things you want to achieve – your choices matter, and you'll invest in creating plans that get you where you want to go. Without a Why you can waste time, energy, resources and opportunities. To really succeed, your Why should be personal and emotional, because it will have to sustain you through everything you face until you finally find the success you've been working for.

Once you have identified your Why, remember to keep it in the forefront of your mind and your life. Remind yourself of your Why at least once a day, and revisit it in case it needs to change in some way to keep pace with your progress. Remember your Why isn't about material things – it's about the difference that material things can make to your life when you are successful. Your Why is your reason for getting out of bed, and while you won't get out of bed for a fancy car, you may get out of bed to enjoy the family road trip you can take in that car, and revel in the pleasure of being able to do something good for the people you love, because you identified your Why and kept sight of it all the time.

Overcoming Negativity

Now you've taken the positive step of identifying your Why, you need to be aware of the negative beliefs that are also being held inside you. This is the #1 source of procrastination, and that's basically what procrastination is: putting things off and not taking action because of a fear or negative belief that you can't achieve your goal. It may be that you're afraid of failure, or it could be that you don't believe you are worthy of having success, or it could even be that you just don't know what your "WHY" is (if that's the case, find one!). I'm here to tell you right now that YOU ARE worthy of success and achieving everything you've dreamed of! Don't let anyone tell you otherwise, including yourself.

Take a moment to close your eyes, take a deep breath, and say, "I am completely able to achieve [state your goal here]." Take note of what negative thoughts you feel, if any, when you say this. This will help you identify what negative beliefs about yourself are inside you. Identify them, write them out, and then write out an opposite positive belief that you can replace it with. Write out all of these new positive statements and keep them next to your "reasons why" statements so you can read them over EVERY day and reprogram your thinking. By doing this, you will set the stage for a VERY productive life where nothing can stop you and procrastination will be no more.

Carry this over to every aspect of your thinking. If you think negatively, turn that thought into a positive one. If you can just see you are going to fail, see yourself succeeding instead. Change your vocabulary around and ditch those negative words, because they are holding you back. Don't say 'I can't do this,' say 'I can do this.' Or if you're not quite ready for that yet, say 'I will be able to do this soon.'

Have faith in yourself, and believe that you can succeed, because if you don't believe in yourself, you are setting yourself up for failure. And if you have no faith in your abilities, other people will pick up on that too, and feed your fears. One of the best things you can do as you move toward your goals is surround yourself with people who believe you can succeed and who will support you in a positive way. People tend to spend time with people like themselves. If you want to attract positive people into your life, you need to be positive yourself. You are your own best advertisement, so cultivate an attractive, upbeat attitude. Straighten up, smile, and look like you can do anything you set your mind to. Now believe your own publicity and get out and do just that!

Take a while to practice your positivity before moving on to the next chapter. Your future self will thank you for it!

Chapter 3: The Importance of Building Routine Habits

Now that we've helped you to get rid of your main sources of procrastination, let's move on to the next part of this quest for productivity, because getting your mindset in the right place is only half the battle. The other side of the productivity coin is all about TAKING ACTION. And the best way to do that is to build solid, regular habits that you can follow and stick to day in and day out. I'm talking about habits that will enable you to stay on top of your goals and to-dos every day, week, and month.

Human beings are creatures of habit. Many of the things we do, we do unconsciously – without actively thinking about what we're doing or why. This is particularly true where small everyday tasks are involved. Think about your routine as you get ready for work. The odds are pretty good that you perform the same tasks in the same way each and every day; it's a comfortable pattern that you're used to. Adding something new to that normal routine – taking five minutes to do some stretching, for example – can feel like it throws everything else off. And if something is taken away from that normal routine – let's say you miss that morning cup of coffee – and chances are that you'll notice that absence quite a bit.

Habits can be positive or they can be negative. Exercising is a habit, but so is smoking! It's important to remember that every habit began with a choice. At some point, you decided you were going to allow a behavior or thought pattern to be part of your life. You have the ultimate control over your habits. If a habit is making you happier and healthier, by all means keep it. If a habit isn't working out so well for you, it's probably time to let it go.

When you have a regular routine of positive habits in place and protect it conscientiously, you are protecting yourself from all the outside distractions in life that seep in and knock you off course. The great thing about building productive habits is that the more you do them, the more natural they feel and the harder it is to stop doing them! We're all about building GOOD habits here, not bad ones!

Willpower alone is not enough to guarantee success, although to succeed at anything, you need a certain amount of willpower. It's a case of planning for success, and the way to do that is to cultivate good business habits and establish a routine that will keep you going and keep you achieving when willpower is in short supply. Willpower is finite – there will come a time when your supply has dwindled to nothing, and that's when habit will kick in and carry you through.

Bear in mind that developing habits to the point where they'll kick in when we're too stressed, tired, or busy to consciously make good choices takes some time. Luckily, it takes less time than you might think. Cognitive scientists –the people who study how our behaviors change brain activity - have found that it takes a little over six weeks of daily practice for a new activity to become an established habit for most people. So if you're feeling overwhelmed about making lifestyle changes, remember this: after only about a month and a half of daily practice, your new organized, productive life will feel completely natural to you!

Throughout the rest of this book I'm going to share 17 core

habits and techniques (or as I like to call them, "productivity hacks") that you can easily implement in your life. When you do this, you'll find that you're completing your daily activities and tasks better. If you want to become more successful, jump start your career path, or even start that business you've always wanted to start, these are the changes you need to make.

I've structured this book so each productivity hack can be mastered independently. You don't have to go through the text in order, although developing one habit can make being successful with the other habits easier. Every one reading this book will have their own unique areas where they're struggling and other areas where they feel strong and confident. Celebrate your strengths, certainly, but concentrate your efforts on those areas where you're weakest.

If you have a trusted mentor, friend, or advisor who you can rely on to speak to you kindly and with honesty, you may want to share this journey with them. Let them know your goal of becoming more organized and productive. They may have insights and guidance that will help you be successful as you set about transforming yourself. It can be hard for us to see ourselves objectively, so having a good-hearted person to act in this role is a real gift. Having the support and encouragement of friends can make it easier to achieve your goals.

In much the same vein, free yourself from negative people's company and commentary while you undergo this transformation. You don't necessarily have to end relationships, but give yourself the gift of space while you're developing your new healthy habits. Remember, it takes about six weeks for a new positive behavior to become part of who you are as a person. After you've worked with these skills and have seen the real beneficial change they've made in your life, it won't matter what the negative people in your life have to say – you'll know what's working for you and how good it feels to be productive and organized!

This will show you how to stop saying "I don't have enough time!" and how to make time for yourself! By following these principles you'll also end up feeling a lot less stressed and cluttered. You'll be a productivity powerhouse so that no matter what you have going on in your life, you will be able to get everything done that needs to get done!

So let's jump right in and get started!

Chapter 4: 17 Habits That Will Make You Organized & Productive

In the tech world, the term hack is used to refer to a quicker, simpler way to do something in order to get desired results. It's a useful term in software development, but it's even more appealing when applied to our everyday life. We can use habits to program our brains to give us the desired results we want – in this case, behaviors that result in greater organization and productivity. You can use these behaviors to better manage your personal life, your professional career, and even help you achieve your fitness and financial goals.

There are seventeen productivity hacks outlined in this section. Seventeen is a number rich in symbolism: since Biblical times, the number seventeen has been said to represent complete victory. Since our goal here is complete victory over procrastination, disorganization, and the other negative habits that have been keeping you from your destiny as a successful person, it's an ideal number of positive habits to develop.

We're going to look at these habits in some detail, and give examples and techniques to help you get it right, as well as explaining why you need to cultivate these particular habits. Work through them, but don't try to do everything at once. Rome wasn't built in a day, and if you try to take too much on board in one go, you could end up missing out on something vital to your success. This is a marathon, not a sprint to the finish line, so pace yourself, and be sure you understand why these habits are important, as well as how to incorporate them into your life.

Habit 1: Set SMART Monthly, Weekly and Daily Milestone Goals

To enjoy a more organized, productive today, you have to know what you want to accomplish tomorrow, next week, next month, and even next year. This long-term perspective is tremendously important.

Remember the time we spent going over identifying your Why? Your Why represents long-term goals. You'll have the most motivation every day when you have a strong long-term goal in place. Your Why may take several years to achieve – particularly if your Why includes things like providing well for your family, a task that can take decades - but there are several components to this that take place on a much shorter timeframe. Knowing where you'd like to be in a year makes it easier to understand what you need to be doing each month. Once you've identified what needs to happen in a month, you'll be able to plan out your weekly and daily tasks much more effectively and be prepared for anything that might arise.

So each week, you need to give yourself some time to sit down and plan out what high-level milestones you want to accomplish in the upcoming month and week, then break those down into smaller milestones by the day.

Introducing SMART Goal Setting

A great way to make productive use of your time is to use the SMART goal setting methodology. SMART goal setting was identified in 1981 by George Doran, Arthur Miller and James

Cunningham, who wrote about the concept in Management Review. The trio introduced the SMART framework as a way to articulate goals that can actually be accomplished.

Success isn't a one-time endeavor: you must win a number of small victories, each one building on previous successes. SMART goal setting provides an easy framework to follow for setting goals that you can realistically achieve. Every time you meet a goal you set for yourself, you'll find your self-confidence building. With practice, you'll find you develop a deeper understanding of what your capabilities truly are. This is an essential element of becoming your most productive self.

SMART: Specific, Measurable, Attainable, Realistic, Time-Based

The SMART goal-setting acronym stands for: Specific; Measureable; Attainable; Realistic; Time-based. To qualify as a useful goal, your objective must meet all five of these qualities. There are variations on this theme, but these are the most popular ones, and the ones that have stood the test of time.

Here's how to get the SMART goal setting tool working right for you, using each of the elements to make sure your goals are clearly defined.

Specific

When your goals are specific, there's a much greater chance of actually accomplishing it than if they are vague or merely generic. So you if you just say you "want to lose weight", that's a very generic goal. Instead, make it more specific like "I'll work out 3 days a week and eat healthy meals every day to lose weight." That's much more specific.

One way to make sure your goal is specific is to make sure that there are identifiable elements in the goal. Who is doing what?

When, and where will it happen? In the example above, I (the who) will work out (what) 3 days a week (when) and eat healthy meals (what) every day (when). All of these are aimed at the end goal, which is to lose weight. This example can be applied to any sort of goal, whether it's related to business or lifestyle.

Measurable:

Make sure your goal is measurable, and that you have something concrete to assess your progress with. With the weight loss example, you'd say I want to lose "10 pounds within 1 month". There is a saying that 'If you can't measure it, you can't manage it,' and this is certainly true of goals. You need something tangible with which to quantify your goal, therefore you need a way to manage it.

Think about how you'll track your progress toward your goal. There are simple approaches you can use. For example, if your goal is to work out three days a week, making a note on your calendar after every gym session is an easy way to record your progress. Technology can be your best friend: wearable fitness trackers, smartphone apps, and online calendars can all be used to track your daily efforts and serve as a log of how consistently you've applied yourself over the course of time. Seeing a chart or graph that visually portrays what you've done can be very motivating – more than one person who's committed to a new fitness regime, for example, has confessed to not skipping a workout specifically because they didn't want that 'day off' to show on their fitness tracker's reports!

Attainable

For best results, all of the goals you set for yourself must be based in reality. We're limited by what's physically possible, and there's only 24 hours in every day. Setting goals like "I'm going to lose 100 pounds by Friday!" or "I'm going to put in 50 hours of overtime every week until my bills are completely paid off!" is a recipe for failure. Trying to achieve the impossible results in nothing but frustration.

As you contemplate a prospective goal, ask yourself does this goal feel attainable? Again, be realistic: you want to be sure that the goal is something that you can do. Set goals based on your current circumstances. If you haven't gotten off of the couch for three years, a goal of running a marathon at the end of the month isn't based in reality.

If a goal you set seems way too far out of reach, then it will actually demotivate you instead of inspiring you. You want to set a healthy attainable level where it's just enough progress to be a "win" for you, while also not too stressful or far out of reach. Instead of declaring that you're going to run a marathon, it may be much more realistic to plan for a 5k!

At the same time, the goals you set shouldn't be so easily attainable that success is assured long before the deadline is reached. Walking across the parking lot is much easier than training for a 5k, but it's an effort that will do little to help you move toward your goal of greater overall fitness. Growth does require some effort.

Be sensible. If the goal compromises your health or safety, or causes too much stress in the achievement, then it is not strictly speaking attainable. If a goal requires no effort for you to achieve it, you're not going to realize much of a benefit.

Strive to find the point where a goal allows you to grow without putting excessive strain into your life.

Realistic

This is very similar to the previous criterion, basically: is this goal realistic? Is it physically possible for me to lose 10 pounds in one month? Does that fit with my schedule, or do I need to adjust the goal a bit? The goal should stretch your capabilities and inspire you to attain it. However, it should not be so difficult, involved or impractical that you lose your motivation. It's a fine balancing act, and as you become more used to setting goals, you will learn how to tailor them in exactly the right way to suit your personality and your own particular working methods.

Setting realistic goals can be surprisingly difficult. Many of us carry around inside our minds a set of expectations – our idea of how things 'should' be done. These 'shoulds' are often based on what we see on TV, online, or on social media. It's important to remember that those images aren't necessarily very realistic. People have a tendency to put their best face forward on social media – while you're oohing and aahing over Facebook pictures of their amazingly organized closets, for example, they're not showing you the fact the garage is overflowing with junk!

If you find you're consistently not achieving the goals you set for yourself, it's a good idea to consider how realistic you're being in your objectives. It's okay to reset goals to better align with your current reality. Once you start hitting those benchmarks, you can readjust again, setting a new set of goals that moves you closer to your ultimate aspirations.

Time-based

Your goal should have a specific time frame attached to it. Otherwise, you'll have no real driving force to get it done. Set the time line with a sense of urgency, but make it achievable, so there is no danger of panic setting in. It's counter productive if you are so distracted by the fear of missing your deadline that you cannot concentrate on achieving the goal you've set for yourself.

It's good to have a variety of deadlines in your life. For example, drinking eight glasses of water can be a daily goal, while working out three times a week is a weekly goal, and competing in the 5K could be a monthly goal. You know you best! If competing in a 5K in a month isn't realistic, adjust that goal – perhaps a six month deadline is a better target. The key is having a specific goal deadline to work toward, and to consistently make progress toward it.

Again, in the weight loss example you would specify when your goal deadline is to lose 10 pounds: 1 month, 2 months, etc? Then give it a specific date like August 10, September 30, etc. Keep it realistic, but also have a clearly defined time frame to work within.

Integrating SMART Goals Into Your Life

By setting SMART goals, you'll have clear guidance on what you can achieve. And of course, you don't have to set NEW goals every week. It all depends on what you're trying to achieve in life, your schedule, and how much you want to accomplish each month and week. In the weight loss example, you could make it your goal to lose 10 pounds in 1 month, so every week you could check in on your progress and make it your goal to lose 2 - 3 pounds every week.

You don't need to work through the items in the order they are set down here. If you find it easier to define your measures first, start with that. Many business experts and motivational consultants consider that to be the most important part of the goal setting process, but whatever works best for you is fine. It's not a rigid structure, rather a framework to help you to identify and set clear and achievable goals to help you to organize your day and your life.

Once you've listed out your goals for the month and week, break them down into smaller milestone chunks by day, so you know exactly what needs to get done each day to reach your overall goals. It's no good setting goals if you then forget all about them – you need to revisit them and check on progress at least once a day, or however often you feel you need to.

Habit 2: Rise early, reflect, and review your routine daily

There is a timeless saying that the early bird gets the worm. When it comes to time management and productivity, this is definitely true. The earlier you accomplish your tasks for the day, the earlier you get to relax and have more free time. This technique is all about using your time and energy in the most efficient way possible.

We only have 24 hours in a day, and in that day we only have so much energy. Both the hours in the day and your personal energy levels are finite – you cannot continue to draw on them when there is nothing left. And that could mean the difference between snagging the deal and missing out on the opportunity, just because you hit the snooze button once too often!

The most successful people in the world realize this and have found ways to get the most out of their time and energy every day.

Understanding what early means

The clock is the same for everyone, but we all have unique schedules based on our workplace, family needs, and personal preferences.

As human beings, we're subject to our biorhythms, a set of inherent cycles in our life which regular our energy levels, memory, creativity and more. You've heard people say they're a night owl? They know that their abilities peak after dark. Other people are at their best in the wee hours of the morning.

Ideally, you'll want to structure your day in a way that aligns with your own personal biorhythms – trying to do a great job in an early morning shift can be very hard for a night owl, because their body is demanding sleep at that time!

That being said, everyone can benefit from extending the number of hours they're awake and active each and every day. Getting up early means getting up early relative to your usual routine. If your current situation has you waking up at seven a.m. to start your day, start setting the alarm for six. If you're starting your day at five p.m., aim for 4 p.m. instead.

Get up early

"Getting up early," means waking up in the morning with enough time to start your day right and NOT in a frantic, hurried rush to work like most people do. You need to give yourself enough time to start your morning right and prepare for your day. Simply transitioning from a sleeping state to alert wakefulness takes some time. Neuroscientists have found that becoming truly awake takes the average person at least half an hour.

Physical activity is one of the best ways to transition from a sleepy state to a more alert mindset. Make time for some stretching exercises and maybe a little yoga, to wake yourself up thoroughly. Getting out in the fresh air is great for all of your senses.

If your schedule allows and the weather's agreeable, make outdoor activity part of your daily morning routine. Even something as simple as stepping out on the balcony to watch the sunrise can be beneficial, particularly if you do it each and every morning. You're training your brain to recognize the cues that you're about to have a productive day! This will enable you to be in a positive mindset for the rest of the day.

Practice getting up early

If the mere thought of getting up early gives you sleepless nights, you need to get some practice in! Set yourself a challenge of getting up 15 minutes earlier than usual for a week, and help yourself to achieve that by moving the alarm clock away from the bed so you have to get out of bed to silence it rather than just hitting the snooze button. By the end of the week, you should find it easier to get up, because you're going to be more tired than usual, so you should drop off to sleep more easily. Now set the alarm for 15 minutes earlier, and continue until you are getting up a whole hour earlier than normal.

However, if you're still struggling, stay with the 15 minutes for as long as you need to. This exercise is about disciplining yourself to start the day earlier so you can prepare yourself for it before you start work, and achieve more when you do. It doesn't matter how long it takes you to get into the early rising habit, as long as you get there in the end.

Getting up earlier is easier when you sleep well. Banish screens from your bedroom for at least an hour before you go to sleep. Our brains need time to unwind; it is impossible to be plugged in all of the time. Staying up late to answer one more email or read another report can actually be counterproductive – the efforts you're putting in late at night are robbing you of your ability to excel the next morning.

Reflect and meditate

As a part of waking up early, reflecting on your life goals and spending time on your self development is VERY important. When you get up in the morning you should make time to take a look at yourself and reaffirm your self-worth and your beliefs about yourself. This makes a HUGE difference on your attitude for the rest of the day and can start you off in a very empowered state of mind to accomplish a lot.

It can help to add visual reminders to your environment that remind you to reaffirm your goals on a daily basis. One way to do this is to write some of your goals and self worth statements on small pieces of paper that you post in your bedroom and bath. As you go about getting dressed and prepared for the day, you'll see these reminders. Read them out loud. The process of hearing your positive vision for your life will help it become a key part of your thought process for the coming day. It will help you stay focused.

Use this quiet, personal time to examine your life goals and any affirmation statements that you may have wrote about yourself. Now I'm not going to get all religious on you, but I also believe in God or a "higher power" that created us to succeed and wills good things for us in life. By believing in something as powerful as this or something similar and reminding yourself of it every day, it helps lay a solid foundation for success.

Everyone needs something to have faith in, even if they only have faith in themselves. However, many successful people are also spiritually aware, whether they believe in God or in some other higher power. It seems to follow that when you have something to believe in, you find it easier to believe in yourself and your own abilities.

Do something with the time gained

Once you've established the early rising habit, put it to good use and do something productive with the time gained. It need not be anything work related, but it should be something concrete, other than preparing your mindset for the day ahead and reflecting on what you want to achieve, and the progress of your goals.

Give yourself something to look back on at the end of the day, so you can say, 'I wrote that blog post/ read that chapter in the book/ did that research because I was disciplined enough to get up early and get things done.' Try to pick activities that you enjoy and feel good about doing. This makes it easier to integrate it into your daily routine.

Write down what you accomplish during your 'extra' morning time. After a week, you'll be surprised how many extra things you've managed to slip into your day, without really trying!

Review your tasks for the day

You also want to wake up early so that you have time to review those tasks you actually need to accomplish for the day. This will make sure you don't start off the day in confusion or unclear vision on what needs to be done. You want to have a laser sharp focus on what you're achieving for the day! You can do this every morning by keeping your tasks in a to-do list or a calendar or planner, which we'll cover more in the next sections ahead.

Obviously, things are likely to happen during the day which will interfere with your plans and may even mess up your whole calendar. However, if you are clear in your mind about the day's tasks before you actually commence your working day, disruption can be kept to a minimum. Each day, anticipate something going wrong and make sure that you prioritize the day's tasks into order of importance. Then if there are problems, or if something urgent comes in or someone calls in sick, you've covered the most important stuff. Prepare for the worst and hope for the best – and if you really want to organize your day, start that preparation before the working day begins.

Make time for breakfast

You've heard it all before, but that's because it's worth repeating over and over – breakfast is the most important time of the day. After the long night with no food, when your body has worked to repair and renew cells as you sleep, your body needs nourishment and so do you, if you are going to be as productive as you can.

Trying to put in a full morning's work without eating breakfast is like trying to run a car that has run out of gas – it isn't going to happen. After being asleep for up to 8 hours, the body's glucose levels are low, and glucose is important for cognitive function. Your brain needs food in the morning, just as the rest of the body does, if you are going to be productive.

Any old glucose will not do though. You could eat a doughnut and it will give you a glucose hit, but in 20 minutes to half an hour, you'll need another one. Or you can eat a bowl of oats or a banana, and that will give you a slow release of glucose over time, to keep your brain fed and your productivity at its peak. A healthy breakfast will also give your metabolism a boost, and that will give you more energy.

So, you need breakfast to boost your brainpower and cognitive function, and to give you the energy to face the day ahead. If you can't face a big breakfast in the morning, just have some fruit, or make yourself a smoothie. A single banana will give your brain the glucose boost it needs and keep up your energy levels until lunchtime. There's certainly food for thought here!

Getting up early, taking the time to revisit your goals and reflect on them, planning the day ahead and eating a healthy breakfast will give you a great start to the day, every day. Being able to take your time to get ready for the working day will help you to be more organized and increase your productivity, so be an early bird and be more successful in your business and in your life.

Habit 3: Prioritize using the 80/20 rule

Have you ever heard of the 80/20 rule? It's a great philosophy to keep in mind on a daily basis and really helps you to get things done!

Basically, it is explained like this: 20% of the tasks you do will accomplish 80% of your overall progress. Stated another way: In the midst of all the to-dos you have on your list, there is a chunk of them (20% of them) that carry the most weight in bringing you the most progress forward.

Because of this, you'll want focus on those top tasks FIRST as they will catapult you to success quicker than if you focused on the tasks that carry less weight and power to accomplish your goals.

The 80/20 rule is also known as the Pareto Principle, after the Italian economist Vilfredo Pareto. In 1906, he came up with a formula to illustrate how 20% of the population owned 80% of the wealth. In the 1930s and 1940s. Quality controller Joseph Juran discovered that the principle applied to quality, and that 20% of goods caused 80% of problems. He dubbed it 'The vital few, and the trivial many,' and experts in all areas have since discovered that the 80/20 rule works for them too.

So for example, let's say you want to clean your entire house this week. There are many rooms and messes to clean up, so where do you start? Using the 80/20 rule, you'd identify what actions would carry the biggest influence in getting your house clean. So, cleaning up the big mess in the living room where everybody walks and sits would be a much more pivotal accomplishment instead of doing something minutely smaller first, like straightening the pictures on your wall or wiping the windows down. You see what I mean? You focus on the BIG tasks first when you have the most energy at the beginning. You can apply this way of thinking to ANYTHING in life. Whether it's starting a business, managing projects at work, or prioritizing your daily schedule. By managing your day in this way, you'll always be able to make big leaps forward in your daily progress.

Understanding the 80/20 Rule at Work

The 80/20 rule works for just about everything, and it works in organization because it helps you to focus your efforts on the vital few – the 20% of your daily tasks that yield 80% of your results. That to-do list you have – 20% of it is going to account for 80% of your productivity or output.

To make it easier to understand, assume that you have 15 items on your list. That means that 3 of them are the most important ones, because they will account for 80% of the day's progress.

You should be able to identify those tasks from the list. If you're running a website or a publication, for example, the three things that are likely to get the biggest results for you are writing content, getting advertising and interacting on social media. So those are the things you should concentrate on first.

They deserve the most of your time, because they will repay you with the highest rewards, both in income and job satisfaction. If anything has to get left until another day, it shouldn't be one of those main items on the to-do list, because those are the vital few, as opposed to the trivial many.

Telling the Vital Few from the Trivial Many

One of the biggest roadblocks that people encounter that keeps them from being truly productive is an inability to tell which tasks are the vital few and which are the trivial many. It can feel like everything on your agenda is vital, and that no single task can go undone without drastic consequences.

If this is the situation you're in, the first step is to make a list of everything you consider absolutely vital. For each task, estimate how much time it will take you to complete the task to the necessary standard. Then total up your list. It's not at all uncommon for people to report that to do everything they need to do, it will require 12 to 15 hours – in an 8 hour work day.

The fact is that being organized and productive requires accepting limits. When you have eight hours to work, you can complete eight hours worth of tasks. Choices have to be made. Some tasks will have to wait; some tasks may need to be delegated to other team members. If you have a positive relationship with your supervisor, it's a good idea to check in periodically and make sure you're prioritizing your efforts in the way they'd like you to: it may be that the item you're sure is high priority may not be as important to them. Simply having that clarified can free up a lot of time and lower your stress levels, with the end result of making you even more productive.

Most managers would agree that the vital few are the tasks that put the most money in the bank account, or bring the most people to your website. Most of the time, you will be easily able to identify these things, or you will experience a 'gut feeling' that guides you. The remaining 20% are tasks that contribute indirectly to the company's profitability. They're still important, but they're not as vital as the cash-generating activities that keep the business afloat. When you can consistently identify the 20%, your productivity and profitability will increase exponentially.

Some of the more minor tasks – the trivial many - can be rolled over so they don't take up so much of your time. Things like emails, for example. Don't keep your personal email account open all the time – log into it at certain designated times during the working day, then read and respond to emails in one session, rather than breaking off from one of your vital few tasks to answer an email that just pinged in. If that happens 10 times a day or more, that's eating into the more productive working time, and it could result in something important going unfinished.

Social media has become more and more central to our lives, but it is a major time waster. Research has shown that people chronically underestimate how long they're on Facebook. The typical social media platform is designed to keep you on the site as long as possible – that maximizes the advertising opportunities that can be shown to you, which is how Facebook, Pinterest, Instagram and other sites make their money. If you're using social media for work purposes, try to schedule that activity during specific times of day, and stay off of those sites during the remainder of the day. As for your personal social media use, it's best to keep that strictly separate from your work life. While it may be entertaining to see what your friends are sharing on Instagram, it's certainly not helping you be more organized and productive!

Understanding 80/20 as a Business Leader

As you become more familiar with the 80/20 rule, you will be able to apply it across the board in your business, and make your day more organized and productive. Concentrate on the vital few services that generate the most interest and income, and leave the rest out of the equation. Identify your vital few skills from all the things you do, and use them more. If there are jobs you do that can be done by absolutely anyone, delegate them. You want to save your time and energy for those jobs that can only be done by you.

Ensure that the 20% (or thereabouts) of your customers who account for 80% of the turnover get the most attention, and don't chase after the Customers From Hell who are never satisfied, no matter what you do for them. You'll be surprised by how many times the 80/20 rule will come to your aid, once you admit it into your working life.

Habit 4: Use calendars, checklists, reminders to manage your daily tasks

If forgetfulness is a problem for you, take heart – you're not alone. In 2014, the Wall Street Journal ran a major story detailing how often people misplace objects, lose track of time, and forget about their commitments.

Calling it a breakdown of the interface of attention and memory, the Wall Street Journal goes on to specify exactly how much time is wasted looking for lost items and scrambling to get tasks completed after the deadline has blown by. For most people, it's at least 15 minutes a day, and it can easily be more. Do the math and you'll soon see what a big problem forgetfulness can be: at just 15 minutes a day, you spend more than an hour of every work week simply trying to find things!

The reason we forget so many things is the fact we live in an overwhelming environment. From the moment we wake up until we close our eyes at night, we're bombarded with a steady stream of messaging demanding our attention. Our brains can't necessarily tell if the news report about a celebrity breakup is any more or less important than the story about a huge change in your industry – it just uses up valuable energy trying to absorb and understand everything it's presented with.

In the midst of all the daily tasks you need to complete, it's frighteningly easy to lose track of everything you want to accomplish, every working day. This is why it's critical to set up a system for yourself where you can easily visualize and track your progress on a monthly, weekly, and daily basis. This will ensure you don't lose sight of anything, so that nothing falls off your radar.

Luckily, there are a number of tools designed to help you keep track of your activities. You can either buy them, or produce your own, customized calendars, planners and checklists. The choice is entirely yours, but make sure that the organizational tools you choose are right for your business and your working methods.

Calendars

Buy or print out a calendar for the next few months, and enter your high-level goals and deadlines on the relevant days. You can easily just Google "PDF calendar" and find one to print out in a matter of seconds. You can use this calendar to visualize your business roadmap and organize your monthly and weekly tasks. Don't get too detailed with the daily tasks on here, this is more for a high level view of things so you don't get overwhelmed.

You'll also want to add national holidays to the calendar – and international holidays if you work with people in other countries, so you know in advance which days are going to be off the rotation. Some holidays are universally observed, while on others it's business as usual. It helps to know what's coming up over the next few months. Daylight savings time can also be an issue when you work with customers or clients across the country. Not every state observes this time shift; you'll want to check what's relevant to your particular business and make notes appropriately.

You may want to consider using calendar software such as

Office 365 or Google Calendar to keep everything together online, and even set up alerts for appointments and events and deadlines. It's a particularly good idea to make use of the alert features, which can send you an email or text as an event draws near. Don't set an alert for everything in your calendar – that's a surefire recipe for overwhelm. Save alerts for those high priority items you absolutely, positively can't afford to miss.

However, it's still a good idea to have a hard copy version – it's much quicker and easier to scan over a calendar that's actually in your hand, and you're more likely to spot mistakes or discrepancies if you're looking at a printed version. Articles about writing always advise writers to print out their pieces when they get to the editing stage, as it's much easier to pick up on mistakes. The same goes for calendars.

Planners

Planners are more useful for remembering the nitty-gritty, day to day and week to week tasks that need to be done. The great thing with planners is that you can produce as many as you want, without confusing the issue. If you employ people, each person can have their own planner. If you have clients, you can produce a separate planner for each client.

Having a master planner that incorporates all the relevant information for each employee or client is also a good idea. That way you can see when two or more major deadlines are going to fall on the same day, or that multiple employees are all planning to be out of the office at the same time, leaving you short staffed. The master planner should be reviewed at least weekly, so you're never surprised by any events.

A planner will help you to schedule your working hours so you can get the most productivity from them. While it doesn't need to be cast in stone, planning out your time effectively before you begin your working day will give you an operational framework to work with. Make sure to put regular, recurring events into your planner; things like staff meetings and quarterly reviews take time and need to be accounted for. Always be realistic over time scales – if you think something will take 30 – 45 minutes, allow one hour, rather than having to play catch up for the rest of the day. Nothing is more demoralizing than spending the working day feeling you are under achieving, when all that really happened was that you were too optimistic with your timings.

Use to planner to schedule productivity-boosting activities into your day. No one can produce at optimum levels for hours on end without taking a break. That's just not how humanity works. Build breaks into your schedule: fifteen minutes to stretch your legs and get away from the computer can do more to boost your productivity than you'd ever imagined.

So, use a planner, but don't let it be a weapon to beat yourself up with when things don't quite work out the way you expected. It's all good productivity training, which will help you to estimate your timings more accurately in future. With all productivity tools, you need to be positive in your approach to using them. You haven't failed if it takes you 75 minutes to complete a task instead of 60 – you just need to get your timing right. You've learned a lesson, not missed an opportunity.

These days, there are many online planners and apps, many of which can be used on mobile devices. If you're good with technology, and you can make the most of the various functions available to you, this can be a great aid to productivity. However, you need to make sure that you are actually using the planner to help your business rather than just playing around with the toys that come with it, because you can waste a lot of time that way if you're not disciplined. Again, make use of alerts, both for yourself and your team members. This will free you from the need to continually check the planner, while still realizing the benefit of having everything written down.

Checklists and reminders

For a more detailed daily view of things, consider getting a good "to-do" app that lets you make checklists for tasks and sends you reminders on your smart phone when things are due. There are tons of apps out there for this, so take do some research and find one you like. Of course, you can always use the good old fashioned route of using a physical notepad planner, but some people prefer to use apps since they're so much cleaner and easier to use. Apps are also great because they usually have built in reminder features. This is really helpful to remind you when things need to be done in the midst of a busy schedule! Checklists can also help build up momentum and keep up your enthusiasm up, as each time you check off tasks from the list it gives a sense of accomplishment.

If you prefer to do a written checklist without the benefit of an app, it's quite easy to do and it's time well spent since it helps you to focus your mind totally on the task in hand. Another bonus with checklists is that they help you to stay consistent, since you work through the same list every time you do the task. And it's also helpful if you want to delegate a task to someone else, because they can see how you do it and maintain consistency.

To produce an effective checklist, first detail all the jobs you do during your day. It doesn't need to be exhaustive, it's just a starting point. Now separate each task, and produce a checklist for it. For example, if one of your tasks is writing blog posts, you may need to check out the latest news for ideas, or research a topic or check out some facts and figures. Then you'll write the blog, and proofread and edit it. Once that's done, you need to choose appropriate images, before posting to the blog and promoting the post on social media.

This is a fairly simple, straightforward example, but it can be applied to any task, any time, whoever is actioning it. Listing the elements of a familiar task is also a good way to identify where changes can be made for better organization or increased productivity. And a checklist is a good training resource for new employees or existing employees wishing to expand their skills base. There are so many good things about using checklists, you'll wonder why you didn't implement them much sooner!

No matter how familiar you are with your work schedule and the tasks you perform on a regular basis, bear in mind the old saying 'Familiarity breeds contempt.' Simply because things are so familiar, you can get into a situation where inefficient methods creep in and go unnoticed, causing you to lose production and even money if the problem is allowed to continue unchecked. Setting up calendars, planners, checklists and reminder systems is a good way to examine your working methods and reschedule or rearrange tasks and appointments. If you want to be more organized and productive, you need to make full use of these resources, every single day.

Habit 5: Stay focused on one thing at a time – don't multi-task!

Contrary to what you've probably been told, multi-tasking can actually be very dangerous to your productivity. This is because it spreads your attention thin if you're trying to do too many things at once, and because of that no single task actually gets the time it needs to be completed. Whatever task happens to be next on your list, give your FULL attention to it. It gets done quicker and, above all, it gets done. This will help you accomplish things faster, and the more tasks you accomplish, the more empowered and energized you'll feel.

Imagine how much better that feels as opposed to trying to do everything at once and not getting anything done – this would make you feel demotivated and can make you lose belief in your ability to accomplish things! You really don't want that. Stay focused on what you need to do, get it done, and then move on to the next task, You'll accomplish a lot more doing it this way rather than multi-tasking, and these are just some of the reasons why.

Focus shifts from task to task

When you multi-task, you don't give your full attention to one element. You're thinking about what you're doing now, what you've just moved on from, and what you're going to be moving to next. Your brain is trying to be in three different places at once, and none of those places is a safe harbor for full concentration on the task in hand. So elements get overlooked, rushed, or just not completed properly. Or you make a mistake and have to start over. Sometimes it's best to just concentrate on one thing at a time – particularly when it's business related. And the problem is, if you're a habitual multi-tasker, when you do try to focus on one task, you won't be able to, because your brain is programmed to flit between tasks.

More stressful

Multi-tasking causes raised levels of the stress hormone cortisol. While some stress is a good thing, too much can make you more impatient, impulsive and aggressive, raise blood pressure and put you at risk of cardiovascular disease. So, multi-tasking can cause chemical changes in the brain, which in turn can have lasting effects on both your physical and mental health. And that is certainly not conducive to better organization and higher productivity. Multi-tasking literally messes around with your mind!

It's taxing for the brain

Despite common perception, the human brain is not programmed for multi-tasking. Aside from the chemical changes that take place, brain scan research shows that rather than balancing tasks competently, the brain darts between them, so everything suffers. The brain is happiest when it's concentrating on a series of tasks in succession, one after the other, rather than trying to cope with two, three or even more tasks at the same time. And it's worse when you try to do similar tasks at the same time, such as communication-related tasks such as speaking on the phone and responding to an email. These activities use the same section of the brain, and it competes with itself for priority, which means it gets itself in a mess and nothing gets done properly, if at all.

Reduced efficiency

Research has shown that multi-tasking can actually decrease efficiency by as much as 40%. People work faster, but actually accomplish less, because of the distractions caused as a result of multi-tasking. You are more likely to make mistakes, which may result in the need to go back and start the task again. Also, each time you switch tasks, you have to close off one before you start on another, and this all takes valuable time which can be better utilized on other projects.

All the latest business thinking points to the fact that multi-tasking is inefficient and not conducive to better organization and increased productivity. It's much better for your emotional and physical health to concentrate on one task at a time, and complete that before moving on to the next. Save multi-tasking for your leisure hours when productivity doesn't matter, if you really want to try it.

Rejecting Multi-Tasking Takes Courage

Multi-tasking is a highly-prized behavior in our culture. Look around you on any given day. You'll see countless people trying to complete fundamentally incompatible tasks at the same time, all in the name of efficiency. How many times have you worked out next to that guy at the gym who insists on conducting a conference call while he's on the treadmill? People read and reply to work emails while they're supposed to be socializing with their friends. The behavior has become so ubiquitous that you may feel a little strange when you stop multi-tasking.

It can be weird to be the only person who's not desperately trying to do it all. To counter this, remember that your goal is mindfulness: you want to keep your brain clear and focused so you can be truly productive and organized. Putting all of your attention on reading one report, for example, will allow you to achieve a greater depth of understanding and insight than your colleague who reads the same report while she's making dinner for her kids.

Multi-tasking is a chosen behavior, and so is mindfulness. Remember, you have the ability and permission to make choices that benefit you and move you closer to your long term goals. We all went through times in high school where we had to reject unhealthy peer pressure, whether that meant saying no to drugs and alcohol or refusing to get involved in activities that would get us into trouble. You will experience peer pressure as an adult as well. When people try to encourage you to multi-task, they may be doing so out of a sincere but misguided belief that this will help you be productive. Firmly but kindly stand your ground. Simply saying "Thank you, but I've found this is what works best for me" can stop a lot of that 'helpful' advice in its tracks.

Don't Believe Me? Test It For Yourself

People are very attached to the idea of multi-tasking, and they're reluctant to give it up for fear that their productivity levels will fall off to unacceptable levels. If this is you, I invite you to put the concept to the test. It's a simple experiment. All you need is two days of your time and a piece of paper.

On day one, proceed with your normal routine. Multi-task as you usually do. After you complete a task, write it down on the piece of paper. Only write down completed tasks; partial efforts don't count for this experiment.

On day two, proceed with your normal routine without multi-tasking. Concentrate on one job at a time, and once it is done, write it down on the other side of your piece of paper.

After day two is done, compare the two lists. How many tasks were completed on the first day, and how many on the second? This is an eye opening experiment for many people. If you're still not sure of the concept, try the experiment for a longer period of time – say a week of multi-tasking, and then a week of mindfulness. That should be plenty of time to convince you that it's possible to do more, better quality work when you abandon multi-tasking.

Habit 6: Have an organized place to record your thoughts

As trivial as it may sound, having a way to write things down throughout your day and store your thoughts is a great habit to get into. In life, spur of the moment things always come up, so you have to be ready for that. During your day you may have a new idea, project, or something else come up that you need to write down before you forget about it. This could be for something that needs to be done tomorrow, or next week, etc. What I'm getting at here is that during your day, you're probably pretty busy and so if you don't write these things down when you think of them, you're going to forget about them later. You can look at it as fail-proofing your life! Be ready to adapt to needs as they come up and change course as needed, because it will happen.

Methods To Record Your Thoughts

The world's most creative, productive people all have one habit in common. They go about their day with a way to record their thoughts on them at all times. This can be a small notebook or sketchpad, a phone app, or even a digital recorder. The technology doesn't matter as much as the sense of constant availability. Putting a system in place to record your thoughts is a valuable sort of affirmation: you're taking action that says your insights and inspirations are valuable and worth keeping.

What Types of Thoughts Are Worth Recording?

It makes sense to have a notepad planner or some sort of pad or notebook where you can easily jot these things down on the spur of the moment. You could also use a phone app - it's really up to you and what you are most comfortable with. But once the methodology is covered, what do you actually want to record?

There are many types of thoughts that cross our mind in any given day. Some of these thoughts are mundane items – things like remembering to pick up cat food on the way home from the office. Other thoughts are more inspired, such as an idea for a new product or service for your business. And then there are thoughts that seem important, but you're not quite sure where they fit or what they mean – things ranging from a quote that struck you as particularly profound or a color scheme that caught your eye.

Write them all down. The mundane tasks are easy to address items that can be crossed out once you've dealt with them, and the inspired moments can become action items. The thoughts that you're not sure how to categorize may seem to be valueless – but not so fast! These items are often gold in the mine, waiting to be discovered and put to use. Our minds don't always work in a linear fashion. We have to collect a number of thoughts and ideas before they coalesce into useable insights. Writing these oddball thoughts down provides you with the raw source material you'll be able to make use of later.

Spending Time With Your Notes

Recording your thoughts is only the first part of the process. If you write everything down and never look at it again, your lists are a waste of time. Your thoughts are worth saving; they're worth spending time with.

It is a good best practice at the end of every day, refer back to this list of things you jot down. You can use your mundane tasks to update your weekly/daily to-do checklist as needed. Larger items and goals may need to make it into your planner; at a minimum, give yourself time to give the idea some serious consideration. The ideas that don't seem to fit can go into a file; review this in its entirely monthly and quarterly. Insights may emerge as the concepts aggregate.

 By making this a regular habit, you'll always be organized and on top of things and prevent your schedule from getting cluttered and overrun by new to-dos in life that come up.

You Are Building A Long Term Resource

Insights and action items can be used more than once. You may even find that these things you write down can have multiple purposes beyond the initial obvious applications.

For example, if you have a website, these jottings could form the basis of blog posts, or even e-books. Or you may find them useful to incorporate into training materials for your business. If you don't have your own business yet, look for ways to use these thoughts to develop your professional persona. Penning articles for industry publications or even posting them to your LinkedIn profile can help make you a more appealing candidate as you develop your career.

At the very least, they will help you with future planning and scheduling, so don't just ditch your notes when you've actioned them. Think ahead of the game, and if they are likely to be useful in future, hang onto them.

It may be a useful exercise at the end of each working week to spend some time going over your notes and even editing them into a permanent document on your computer, so that all the notes that may be useful to you in the future are kept together in one easily accessible space. Sometimes, random, spur of the moment thoughts can be very insightful and rewarding, so don't be in too much of a hurry to get rid of them.

Habit 7: Review progress daily and weekly

No matter what your professional goals may be, the ability to accurately assess performance and make recommendations based on observed results will help you achieve them. Many times, professional advancement means taking on roles where you have to oversee other people's efforts and guide them into making more productive choices. The best way to learn how to do this is to practice on yourself, reviewing your own progress regularly.

The Daily Progress Review

Starting each day with a to-do list in place gives you the opportunity to assess your performance each evening. In light of all these productivity hacks and techniques we've reviewed so far, this is another essential habit you'll want to form which will help to tie it all together.

This is most likely the last thing you'll do at the end of each day, and it will help you prepare for the next working day. Just as it's important to start off your day by reviewing what tasks need to get done, it's also just as important at the end of each day to review what you have accomplished and make the necessary adjustments to tomorrow's schedule.

It could well be that maybe you only were able to accomplish 5 out of the 8 tasks you had on your checklist for the day, and that could be due to all sorts of reasons. Maybe you just gave yourself too much to do that day, or maybe an unexpected new event came up in your day that you had to divert your focus and attention to. Whatever the case, it happens. That's why reviewing your day at the end is so important, for these reasons.

A measure of achievement

The daily performance review will help you gauge how much you can handle and accomplish on a daily basis. Maybe you started out giving yourself too many tasks to do in one day. As we've discussed, many people struggle with unrealistic expectations of themselves. If that's the case, you'll start noticing that at the end of each day there were a certain number of tasks you didn't complete. Take note if this is happening a lot, and try to work out why it might have happened. This will help you to analyze your productivity and reflect on what's working for you and what isn't.

The important thing is to reflect and identify where you're hitting roadblocks, and make the necessary changes so that your next day is super productive! Making this a habit will help you grow and become better organized and more productive.

A preparation and planning resource

If there are some tasks that you didn't complete for the day, you'll need to prepare for the next day and make some space for the tasks you didn't finish today. In that case, you'll have to shift everything around. That means going into your checklist, notepad or app and updating the due dates for these tasks you didn't accomplish and moving them to tomorrow's due date instead. Some tasks may need to be moved on another day, or dropped from the immediate schedule altogether.

The point is to have clear action steps for the next day so that when you wake up, you can hit the ground running and know exactly what you need to do. Don't spend valuable production time trying to reschedule tasks that should have been picked up and dealt with in the end of day review.

If you find you're continually needing to reschedule tasks, try scheduling some empty slots into the final days of your work week. That way, when you find you're getting behind, you'll have the time available to complete tasks in a timely fashion. Every organization is different, but most have a pattern of busy and slow days. Knowing you have the ability to postpone some tasks to the slower days can lower your stress levels considerably and still make sure you get all your necessary work done.

The Weekly Performance Review

Reviewing your performance at the end of each day should give you a real sense of how productive you're actually being and how you're progressing toward your goals. That being said, it's still a good idea to do this "reflecting" on a weekly basis too.

Each new week presents an opportunity to make better use of your time and be more productive. When you're creating your daily to do lists for the coming week, be aware of what issues you ran into this past week or what things you didn't accomplish, and think about why that happened. Some obstacles are going to be recurring problems, while other issues are (hopefully) one-time occurrences. For example, if you know your meeting with a particularly chatty client consistently runs a half hour longer than you anticipate, anticipate a longer meeting. On the other hand, the fact a delivery van had an accident and knocked out the power for the neighborhood one afternoon is unlikely to recur and doesn't need to be accommodated in the coming week's schedule.

By reflecting and identifying where you had difficulties, you can create a better strategy for next time and make sure you're more successful. Good questions to ask during this reflection include not only whether you're making good use of your time, but if any of the tasks you're performing can be delegated to someone else so you can engage in more high value work. Check to make sure you're including productivity boosting activities into your schedule. Breaks and continuing education are two items that can help you consistently turn in a better performance. Make sure they appear regularly on your agenda.

When you conduct the weekly review is entirely up to you. You may choose to do it on Friday, at the end of the working week, or on Monday, at the start of the new working week. You could even do it midweek. Whatever suits your schedule and your working methods is the right time for you. Remember this review is not aimed at beating yourself up for lack of progress – it's about identifying where improvements can be made and motivating you to boost productivity and plan more effectively.

Your Growth Journal

It's important to recognize and reflect on the accomplishments you make as you grow more organized and productive. One easy way to do this is to begin keeping a growth journal. This can be very simple: just designate a notebook as the place you record your thoughts and feelings after each week's performance review. Some weeks you may feel really great about what you've accomplished, while other weeks aren't quite as inspiring. Just write down a few sentences about what you're feeling, and put the journal away until it's time to repeat the process next week. At the end of a quarter, read your growth journal. It will show you exactly how far you've come – and you may find that your progress, when viewed over the long term – is very surprising indeed!

Habit 8: Guard your time and stay clear of time wasters!

This may seem obvious, but many people don't even realize how much time they waste doing "useless" things throughout their day. By "useless", I mean doing things that don't move them forward in accomplishing their tasks for the day. This consists of big time wasters like going on social media, watching TV or movies, playing video games or game apps on your phone, or just browsing random things on the internet. Don't get me wrong, these things aren't bad and of course it's good to spend time on relaxing and leisure, but the issue is WHEN you do it. And this is where most people struggle. Some people go straight to social media the minute they wake up, and spend too much time on it throughout the day.

Obviously, this can affect your productivity in several ways. For one, going on social media or doing other mindless things can interfere with your routine habits and disrupt your schedule. If you spend your morning on Facebook instead of planning and reviewing your day, you're already losing the productivity battle. You'll go into your day with a very unclear sense of what needs to be done that day! Secondly, the more time you spend on mindless time consumers, the harder it will be to break the habit of doing it.

Now, I'm not saying going on social media during the day is bad. Instead, you should ONLY do it when it fits around your productivity schedule. If you're in the middle of something important, don't go on social media. If you're taking a 15 minute break and want to clear your head, then it's fine to go on it for a few minutes. But save the bulk of your leisure activities for the end of the day, after you've accomplished all your to-dos for the day. That way you don't have to worry about it and you won't feel guilty about it! Here are some great ways to guard your time.

Turn off the Internet and electronic devices

The best way to stop yourself wasting time on social media and other electronic distractions is to turn them off while you're working. Be firm with yourself, and only turn these devices back on when you have finished what you need to accomplish. If it helps, set yourself a reward scheme as an incentive. After two hours work, you will grant yourself a 10 – 15 minute break when you can check out Facebook, answer some personal emails or text a friend. Or you may decide that when you have written 4 blog posts, you will spend 10 minutes online.

By setting up a reward scheme for electronic distractions, you are boosting productivity in two ways. First of all, you are removing the source of the distraction, then because you are going to reward yourself after a couple of hours work, you're likely to work that much harder and faster. In any event, it's a good idea to take regular breaks after a couple of hours, as your concentration is likely to flag after that time, so it's a great solution.

Be aware social media is designed to keep you engaged

The average American's attention span is less than 8 seconds. A goldfish, on the other hand, has an attention span that averages 9 seconds. We are easily distracted, and the reason for this can be traced almost directly to social media.

Researchers know that human beings will engage in a behavior almost endlessly if they are rewarded at irregularly occurring intervals. This is why slot machines appeal to gamblers: they know if they play long enough, they're sure to be rewarded, if only with a few tokens. Social media works the same way. If you keep scrolling, eventually you're going to find content that entertains you, whether it's a funny meme shared by a friend or a video showing a neat way to use your favorite product.

Your time is worth money to the social media companies. The longer you're on Facebook, Instagram, or Pinterest, the more opportunities they have to show you advertising. That's why they are aggressively and continually adding new ways to keep your attention, from offering many new types of video content to adding in platform shopping options and addictive games.

It's important to remember that your time is worth money to you as well. If you're struggling to put down the phone and get back to work, try putting a dollar value on your social media time. Is it really worth an hour of your pay to look at what's happening on Twitter? Would you rather have that amount of cash or an hour of scrolling through Instagram photos? Having your social media time expressed as an expense can help you realize its true value to you.

Turn off business email alerts

It can be very tempting to leave whatever you're doing and attend to business emails when an alert comes in. That means you're going to spend an average of 10 minutes reading and responding to the email, then you've got to return your concentration to the task in hand. So productivity takes a hit.

Schedule times to answer your business emails – say at the beginning and end of the morning, and the beginning and end of the afternoon. Then you can give your full attention to them rather than interrupting other tasks at random times to attend to emails.

I can already hear you saying that this tip is impossible because you're working on this important project or that very special client just can't be ignored. You're going to need some willpower here. Remember the discussion we had on mindfulness versus multi-tasking? This is the same sort of situation. Immediate responsiveness may look like excellent customer service, but in truth, you're not giving your clients your best possible work when you're rushing to respond to them.

Have you ever wound up in a situation where there's confusion because someone did not read and understand an email before they responded to it? The odds are pretty good that you can say yes to that scenario. By delaying responding to business emails until a designated time, your focus is increased, and mistakes due to an overly rapid reading diminish. Good work takes time. Give yourself and your clients the respect of treating every one of their communications as if it was important and deserved a considered response.

Focus on what you're doing

Okay, the internet is off, and electronic devices are silenced, but if you're still not focused on the task in hand, your productivity is going to suffer. So remind yourself of what you should be doing, and focus your mind on the task in hand. If you're having a problem getting motivated, try visualizing the task. Map out the stages in your mind, and imagine yourself working through those stages until the task is completed. Now imagine how good you will feel when the task is completed and you can tick it off your list. Visualization is a classic anti-procrastination technique, and it will often help you to get started on the project. Once you've made a start, it's easier to keep going and complete the task ahead of you.

Keep a time log

Often, when you think you are working for an hour, you may only spend about 40 minutes of that hour on productive work. Other things like answering the phone, replying to emails, chatting to colleagues and visiting the bathroom can eat into that work time. Try this experiment for a day, to identify where you are wasting time. Have a piece of paper or a document on the computer and list the day in one hour blocks down the left hand side of the page. At the end of each hour, stop what you're doing and look back over the hour. Jot down approximate timings for everything you've done, and then review it.

Are you happy with what you've achieved within the hour, or do you think you could have done better, and produced more? See if you can do better in the next hour, and achieve more. The time log is most effective when it's completed over the space of several days, so don't rush the exercise. Again, remember the time log is not a weapon to beat you with to make you more productive – it's a valuable analysis tool to help you make the best of your time and organize your day more efficiently.

Learn to say no

If you don't feel you need to attend a particular meeting, say so, rather than going along because your boss or a colleague thinks you should. If your time could be spent more productively, say so. You can always send along your contribution with someone else, if you have a relevant point to make. Ask to see the agenda, so you can make an informed decision on whether you need to attend or not.

When you're busy and your colleague wants to chat, tell her you don't have time to stop right now, but you'd love to hear her news at lunchtime, or over a drink after work. Learn to say no, and prioritize your work and yourself. Don't take every phone call – relay messages through other people to save yourself time and distraction. If you're worried that people won't like you if you say no, don't fret – they will respect you for recognizing your responsibilities and knowing your limitations. You are not indispensible – nobody is. The world won't come to a standstill because you refuse to attend a meeting or take a call.

By guarding your time and recognizing how you waste it, you can organize your day much better and boost your productivity. It's not rocket science – minimize distractions, keep yourself focused, answer business emails in blocks rather than randomly and learn to say no to non-urgent tasks and assignments.

Habit 9: Create a reward system for yourself

Encouraging yourself to be more productive *IS* a productive habit. Rewarding yourself for finishing difficult tasks or surviving a hard day without giving up or procrastinating *IS* self-encouragement. It is very important to remember to appreciate your own efforts through rewards, and here's why: this is actually a productivity hack that the most successful and wealthy people do... because it works!

It's a brain hack that actually tricks your brain into wanting to do MORE productive habits because of the rewards to be gained after completing them! Instead of feeling like your tasks are a dreaded responsibility, you'll feel excited to complete them. By doing this, you set yourself up for major success!

It's not all in the mind either – when you do something pleasurable, like rewarding yourself, dopamine is released into the brain, and that stimulates the neural pathways. Your brain effectively becomes a dog who's received a treat for getting his training right – it's anxious to do more to get another reward, and the dopamine hit that comes with it. In fact, over time, the dopamine hit becomes more important than the reward, so the habit of being more productive becomes ingrained, and productivity gets a permanent boost.

Timing Your Rewards

Retail guru Rick Segel famously said, "The behavior that is rewarded is the behavior that is repeated." So if you know you want to consistently repeat a behavior, reward yourself for completing it on a regular basis.

So for example, you could reward yourself to a nice tall latte from your local coffee shop every morning as a reward for waking up early, meditating, and reviewing your tasks for the day. Do this every day and it will set up a spiraling cycle of success, where the more you do it, the harder it will be to break the habit. Pick one productive habit that you can reward yourself for every day, and you will soon see that it will become easier and easier!

You could even have a tiered reward system to match the achievements. The bigger the accomplishment, the greater the reward. Accomplishing the morning routine gets you the latte. For something a bit more of an achievement, say adopting or sustaining a good habit for a week or a month, the reward should be a little grander. That can be something like a special night out at a concert or the movies, or a meal at that fantastic new restaurant you've wanted to try for ages.

Finally, for the really big deal that happens once in a while, reward yourself with an equally big treat. Take a weekend away, buy yourself a new set of golf clubs or some expensive new toy. You deserve it!

Rewards are Extremely Individual

Most productivity hacks are based on some sort of review and/or reward system, and that's because it works! The key to creating an effective reward system for yourself begins with self-knowledge. You have to know what you value and find special. A latte may not fall into your category of a wonderful treat – but what does? If you're going to get more joy out of downloading a new song or going biking after work, make that your daily reward.

Your rewards should be make your life better. Be very cautious of treating yourself with a cocktail at the end of the day – while indulging is fine once in a while, it can get very easy to talk yourself into believing you deserve more and more rewards of this type and before you know it, you're looking at health and relationship troubles. A reward that causes you more life stress isn't actually a reward!

Also be realistic about your budget when choosing your daily reward. Lattes and similar treats can get pricey fast. If one of your goals is to save money and pay down debt, you may want to identify rewards that don't cost so much. Connecting with your favorite friends for a few laughs doesn't have to put you out of pocket and can be a great reward for a week when you've worked to the very best of your abilities.

It's Good To Reward Others Too

Very few of us make it through the day completely on our own. Whether it's the co-worker who lends a helping hand when we really need it or the Uber driver who made sure you made it to your morning flight on time, there are other people who make our lives qualitatively better.

Look for opportunities to surprise these people with rewards whenever you can. This doesn't have to be a big deal – something like a $5 coffee shop gift card can really put a smile on someone's face, especially when they're not expecting it.

You may think rewarding others is all about celebrating them, but in truth, it serves a valuable purpose in your life. There's no better burst of endorphins than the one that comes with knowing you've put a smile on someone's face. The world's a tough place sometimes, and introducing a little kindness into it is a good thing. Besides, interpersonal relationships are really important. When you step up into that leadership role and say to someone "Hey, you matter. You make a positive difference in my life," you're demonstrating that you can see the value in others. This will strengthen the bond you have with that person and help you forge a strong extended network of colleagues and peers.

Habit 10: Learn when to say "No"

Learning when to say "no" to things is probably one of the most valuable lessons you can learn in life. As has been stated before, everyone has just 24 hours in every single day, and there are dozens of different things vying for attention every day of your life. If you said, "yes" to every single thing, nothing valuable or productive would ever get done. You'd be snowed under and demoralized, and you'd spend more time worrying about how you were going to get everything done than actually doing anything!

You need to learn to prioritize things and be careful about what you say "yes" to every day. By learning to say "no" to things that aren't worth your time, you are protecting your success and productivity, and your overall health and happiness.

This can be applied to any aspect in your schedule. As much as your job or occupation is appreciated for its financial benefits, sometimes it is healthy to say no to additional offers if it will cut into your time in an unhealthy way. Time IS money, so you want to protect your time just as much as you would protect your money. If your friend asks you to join a book reading club with them that meets once a week, but you don't have the time for that, it's ok to say no! Learn to protect your time in a healthy way and find the right balance.

Another thing to consider is who you spend your time with. They say you are an average of the 5 people you spend most of your time with. So who are the top 5 people you are around the most? Do they influence you in a positive way or a negative way? Do they instill productive habits in you or destructive habits? Keep this in mind and learn which friends you need to say "no" to.

How to say no graciously

Most people don't say "no" because they think they will offend other people, or they believe their business contacts won't want to deal with them in the future. In truth, how you say no is important, because that could mean the difference between the other person accepting your decision in the spirit it was made, and feeling rejected.

The first thing to remember is that people – especially business people and work colleagues – don't normally ask you to do things on a whim. If they ask you to do something, it's because it needs to be done, and they think you are the best person to do that. That probably makes you feel good, so you also feel bad about refusing the request. However, if you really can't do it, you're going to have to find a nice way to say so.

Don't keep the other person waiting around for an answer – especially if you have made up your mind to say no. That's wasting valuable time when they could be looking for someone else to take on the project. And be sure you explain honestly why you are refusing the request. Whether it's because of other commitments, the anticipated time frame, or you don't feel comfortable with it for some reason, explaining why takes some of the sting out of your answer.

If you can, suggest someone else who may be able to take on the task, or find another way to help them to accomplish their task. Maybe you can delegate a member of your team to help with it. At least if you explain why you can't do it and offer some help in getting the problem sorted, the other person will realize that you are not refusing their request because you are unhelpful.

Once you've made the decision to say no, be resolute. Don't allow yourself to be talked around, or you will lose the respect of your colleagues, and next time they want someone to do something, they'll come back to you, because they will decide that your no really means yes.

Sometimes you have to say 'no' to yourself!

Throughout the course of this book, we've been discussing life hacks designed to make you more organized and productive. These new habits are meant to take the place of your old habits – but old habits can be powerful!

Let's say you've committed to starting each day a little earlier. Waking up an hour early has so many benefits, and you've been diligently getting up with your alarm for the past three weeks. But on the first day of that fourth week, your brain says, "Hey, wait a minute. I'm tired. Sleeping in just one day won't matter all that much!"

A warm, cozy bed is a real temptation. Even though you know intellectually that you're trying to develop a new habit that will improve your life, the mattress is so soft and comfortable that you seriously contemplate hitting the snooze button – three or four times in a row!

This is when you need the strength and determination to say 'no' to yourself. Make no mistake, this can be a big challenge.

The key is to remember you're making changes to improve your life. Ask yourself, out loud, "How will I feel if I stay in this bed all day?" Remember that you're thinking in the long term, as well as the immediate moment. Sleeping in might feel great right now, but later, when you're rushing to make it to work on time, and you've skipped through the helpful, healthy new morning routine you've established for yourself, it's going to be a stressful, unpleasant experience. Contemplating the consequences and realizing you'll be shortchanging yourself of an opportunity to grow and improve as a person can make saying 'no' a little easier.

What does saying "yes" mean?

If you have a problem saying "no" because you're a people pleaser, just stop and think what would happen if you said "yes." Because the truth is, when you say yes to someone else, you're actually saying no to yourself or someone you love. Saying yes could mean you miss out on family time, and that can lead to a build up of anger and resentment which will impact on several aspects of your life, both at work and at home. If saying yes is eating into your relaxation time, you could even be putting your health at risk.

Thinking of the possible personal consequences of saying yes when you really should be saying no should help you to get things into perspective. That will make it easier for you to say no, and it will get even easier with practice.

Factors that influence your ability to say "no".

Some people have absolute no issue saying "no" while other people really struggle with it. If you're in this latter camp, don't beat yourself up for this difficulty. There are several cultural and social factors that make it harder for some people to say "no".

I've talked about being a people pleaser. People pleasers can be either male or female, but they're much more likely to be female. This is because girls are socialized to make sure everyone is happy and getting along nicely – even when achieving this state means this that their own personal goals and desires get pushed to the wayside. If you know this is an issue for you, look into assertiveness training specifically for women. There are many free online resources that can help you overcome the habits you learned in childhood. In the beginning, saying 'no' – especially to people who have only ever heard you say 'yes' – can be very uncomfortable. However, as you grow acclimated to having better control over your own time, you'll find the response feels a little more natural.

Workplace dynamics can also make saying 'no' difficult. The management style of the person you report to can definitely influence how comfortable you are asserting your boundaries. If this is the case for you, observe how your other colleagues handle the situation when they tell the supervisor or manager "no". Emulating the tools and techniques they use may make your efforts at saying 'no' more successful.

Habit 11: Learn how to delegate tasks

There is a very under-utilized tactic that most people forget about or don't even think about: delegating tasks to others. Actually, most people probably WOULDN'T want to do this at first glance. Especially in America, where independence is one of our key values, it's very ingrained in our society and culture to do everything yourself. While this is a very ambitious mindset to do everything yourself, it's also very prohibiting to productivity. Here's why it can actually be very helpful to delegate work to others when needed.

Sometimes you just have WAY too much to do in one day, and in some cases you really can't shift your tasks to later due dates. When this happens, it's very easy to become overloaded with everything you have to do... and then you start to get stressed out, and it's a downward spiral from there. Not a good situation to be in. Thankfully, there are millions of other human beings in the world... and I'm sure some of them could help you out.

So for example, if your day is just way too busy and you still have to clean the house because your in-laws are coming over the next day... you should really consider getting someone else to clean it for you! If you have kids, get them to do it! Give them some sort of incentive to help you out. If you don't have kids, then hire someone to do it – I'm sure you could find a pretty cheap local service or even a college kid who wants some extra cash.

If you're at work and your project list is overloaded, consider outsourcing some of your work to contractors or VAs. You can easily do this nowadays by going on freelancing sites such as UpWork. You'll find tons of people who can help carry your load and make your life easier.

Do you see how helpful it can be to get extra help when needed? Don't be afraid to ask, set aside your pride. Of course, do make sure to thank whoever it is that helps you and let them know you appreciate it.

Delegating allows you to make the best use of your time

It's important to understand the difference between being busy and being productive. When you're busy, you're filling every minute of your day with activity, but that's no guarantee you're moving closer to achieving your goals. When you're productive, your day may be every bit as full, but the work you're doing consistently moves you closer to fulfilling your plan for yourself.

It is much better to be productive than to be busy. When you're looking at your daily to-do list, consider the value of each task. There are some jobs that clearly will move you closer to achieving your goals. For example, if you're trying to grow your business, meeting with a prospective new client is a very important way to spend your time.

But on the same to-do list, you may also have items like call the copier repair service. The copier may very well need repair – but will spending half an hour on the phone trying to schedule a service call do anything to grow your business? The answer here is no: you're not being productive, you're just being busy.

Busy work can and should be delegated. Deciding who to delegate the task to can vary based on who you have available to you; in the case of the one-person shop, finding someone to delegate to may involve bringing in a third party, such as a virtual assistant.

Put a dollar value on your time

If you're struggling with the idea that you should delegate, try thinking about the decision from a financial perspective. There are only so many hours in the day, and obviously you want to realize the maximum amount of money possible from each one.

Some of the activities you do in the course of your day are clearly money makers, while others aren't. Dividing those two sets of tasks are fairly easy. But what happens when you have many tasks that could be potentially profitable? The temptation is to do it all yourself – but as we've discussed, that's not always a wise move.

Make a list of your tasks, and assign a dollar value to each. For example, meeting with the new client could result in a $10,000 sale, delivering a special order to an existing client could net you $2,500, and cold calling could generate up to $1,000 in new revenue on a great day. With the numbers in front of you, deciding what tasks are a priority becomes easier. Remember, you can delegate profitable tasks as well as unprofitable ones – but you'll want to keep the most lucrative projects for yourself. Don't give away the $10,000 meeting to spend the day making $1,000 worth of cold calls!

How to delegate successfully

While you may be unwilling to delegate, nobody can do absolutely everything in a successful enterprise, and the time will come when you have to call on help from someone else. When that happens, being able to delegate successfully is important if you want to maintain standards and keep everyone happy.

Make sure whoever is taking on the task has all the information they need to complete the task competently. Explain what they need to know, answer any questions they may have, then trust to their ability and allow them some freedom. Everyone has their own working methods, and, rather than spelling it all out chapter and verse, allow them some leeway to express themselves and demonstrate their own particular expertise. Make sure they know what your expectations are regarding completion of the project, and then leave them to get on with it.

If you can train yourself to delegate successfully, you'll be among the 10% of management who regularly use delegation as a resource for getting things done. It's a valuable skill to learn, and it will help you to be more organized and productive in your working life, as well as freeing up more leisure time for you to enjoy with friends and family. Shouldn't you be delegating more?

Habit 12: Get enough sleep and exercise

Being organized and productive isn't confined to the workplace and to working hours. It starts at home, with getting enough rest and exercise so that you are fit and healthy and ready to face the challenges the day brings. Sleep and exercise help to sharpen up the mind and improve cognitive function so that you can deal with the challenges that arise during a typical working day.

Sleep deprivation is a big problem for many American adults. The Center for Disease Control has done extensive research on this topic, and found that more than a third of people just aren't sleeping enough. The results of chronic sleeplessness can be catastrophic, personally and professionally. Poor decision making, inattentiveness, diminished awareness, slower response times, and physical clumsiness can all combine to contribute to accidents, particularly while driving.

Americans are also known for leading very sedentary lives. We just don't get out and move very much. Ninety percent of our lives are spent indoors, and most of that time is either spent sitting in a chair or lying in a bed. This has obvious implications for our physical health, particularly the cardio-vascular system. Additionally, as you'll read in this chapter, exercise can impact our mood, critical thinking, and even creativity.

Get enough sleep

While most people today don't go to bed "early", this is something you should try to get into the habit of. The amount of sleep you get is MASSIVELY influential to the amount of energy you'll have for the next day. Sadly, most people get much less sleep than they need. And since you're waking up early in the morning to get a head start on your productive routine, you need to go to bed in time to get sufficient restful sleep.

During sleep time, your body works hard to repair and renew its cells. This is a task that can only be done when you're at rest, because it takes so much energy, and during the day, that energy is taken up with keeping the body functioning healthily and normally. This repair and renewal process also concerns the brain cells. Too little sleep results in impaired memory function and the inability to make rational decisions, and this can affect productivity adversely. If you start the day off drowsy and below par, it's only going to go downhill from there, so make sure you get enough sleep for the sake of your body and your brain.

People who habitually get less than 6 hours of sleep are less productive than those who sleep more, even when they wake up earlier in the morning. Decide what time you're waking up the next morning, and work backwards from there to decide when you need to go to bed. Your body goes through sleep cycles of about 90 minutes, and it's best to wake up at the end of a sleep cycle so you don't feel groggy. So you should either get 6 hours of sleep or 7.5 hours of sleep, depending on what your body can handle. Test it out and see how much sleep your body needs to be at your best the next day.

Screen time and sleep

Television, the internet, and our smartphones are all taking a toll on our ability to fall and stay asleep successful. Sleep researchers have a variety of theories about why this is the case. Some posit that it's exposure to the flickering lights that contributes to insomnia, while others believe that the content we engage with, from an everyday email to a thrilling action adventure movie, that energizes the brain and keeps it active and thinking when it should be focused on relaxing and rejuvenating.

While we are not sure of the exact reason why screen time disrupts effective sleep patterns, we do know that there's a simple way to address the issue. One hour before you plan to go to bed, turn your electronic devices off. Give yourself the luxury of sixty minutes without screen time. This is a great period of time to decompress from your productive day, enjoy the companionship of your partner or spouse, and simply relax. Some people find they sleep better if they engage in gentle exercise or a relaxing bath before bedtime.

Power naps

Try to cultivate the habit of taking a short nap at least once a day, if possible. Research shows that naps increase productivity by at least 40% compared to not getting any form of rest in the day. If you want to have optimum energy and enthusiasm to get through each day it's highly advisable to reward yourself a short powernap if possible – about 25 minutes should be enough.

In fact a 20 minute power nap half way through the working day is more beneficial for alertness and productivity than sleeping for an extra 20 minutes in the morning. Taking a power nap helps you to relax and lowers stress levels, so even if you feel a little drowsy for a few minutes after waking, in no time at all you'll be more alert and more productive.

A doze during the day can also improve your memory and make you more receptive to learning new things. According to research, power napping protects the brain from overload by allowing it to rest and process new knowledge before continuing to work. It can also improve cognitive function by as much as 40%, so the case for taking a power nap is pretty overwhelming.

Embrace the power of exercise

Sleep is wonderful, but it isn't all you need. Human beings were designed to live active, mobile lifestyles. This means exercise is also important, because just as sleep rests and relaxes the brain, exercise can stimulate it in the right way. All parts of the body benefit from exercise, and the brain is no exception. The obvious benefit to the brain is that exercise boosts the circulation, which means that all parts of the body get more blood and oxygen, which means they function more efficiently and stay healthy. So, the lesson would appear to be clear.

Get out there and exercise

When you exercise, even if it's just one time per week, it actually energizes your body and mind. There's something about exercising that has a rejuvenating effect. Many people experience difficulty getting themselves off the couch and going out to the gym or even just outside for a walk or a run. However, every time they actually get up and do something, they feel SO much better afterwards and have renewed energy! If you have trouble getting yourself to exercise, try using the reward system to motivate yourself. Pick a reward – preferably a healthy one - to give yourself every time you complete an exercise session. All in all, if you exercise on a regular basis and incorporate it into your routine, you'll experience more energy, vitality, and productivity in your day.

Ideally, you should aim for a minimum of five 30 minute exercise sessions every week. You don't have to hit the gym if the mere thought of putting on the lycra brings you out in a cold sweat. Do something enjoyable, and do it with someone else, because that way, you're more likely to stick with it. Swimming, walking, cycling and dancing are all sociable, aerobic exercises that you can do with other people, which will motivate you to continue. And the great thing is, none of these exercises requires expensive specialist equipment. The benefits of exercise for mind and body are numerous, so get yourself moving, and boost your productivity at work!

How exercise can make you more productive

Exercise is good for you – everyone knows that. It boosts the metabolism, and helps you to maintain a healthy weight. That means you're less susceptible to lifestyle illnesses such as hypertension, heart disease and diabetes. To be successful in your work you need to be fit and healthy, and exercise can help you to achieve that. Recent research has shown that exercise is good for much more than getting you into shape – it can actually boost productivity levels too.

Boosts brainpower

It's common knowledge that exercise releases 'feel good' hormones to lift your mood, so it's a great help if you're depressed. But scientists now know that exercise has a direct effect on the brain cells. As you get older, the brain has fewer cells, because the body does not generate so many. This is a process known as neurogenesis. The good news is that regular exercise slows down neurogenesis, so as you enter your 50s and 60s, you're likely to have more brain cells than your more sedentary peers. That's going to give you a real edge in the work place, because more brain cells makes for a more efficient brain.

And you don't need to pump the iron in the gym to enjoy this benefit. Moderate exercise such as a brisk lunchtime walk or a refreshing swim will do the trick, as long as you get slightly out of breath. Just 30 minutes of cardio exercise gives the brain a blood and oxygen boost that helps it to perform better. Exercise also releases various chemicals into the brain, such as serotonin, the famous 'feel good' hormone, dopamine, which helps with cognitive function and increases your attention span, and norepinephrine, which also helps you to pay attention, as well as improving motivation and increasing perception.

Exercise also relieves stress and makes you more relaxed, so you are better equipped to cope with problems as they arise. Really, if you want to be more organized and productive, you need to fit some exercise into your day!

Increases energy levels

You might think that fitting exercise into an already crowded schedule would be tiring, but the reverse is actually true. That's because regular exercise stimulates the body to produce more mitochondria. Simply put, that's the stuff in the cells that produces energy, which is why mitochondria is known as the cell's own power plant. This means you have more energy to do what needs doing every day, and your brain also benefits from this increased energy, so it's a win-win situation.

Studies indicate that people who exercise regularly can boost their productivity by as much as 23%, and these benefits spill over and last much longer than the exercise session. That means that when you get home, you'll have more energy for your kids or your significant other, or just to factor in some leisure activities rather than crashing out on the couch as soon as you get through the door.

Builds Relationships

Exercise can also play an important role in our social lives. While some forms of physical activity are definitely solo endeavors, things like running, spin class, and team sports require being around other people. Many of us don't get much opportunity to socialize outside of the office, but we desperately need that interpersonal contact. Having a buddy you see at the gym, even if your conversation never goes any deeper than talking about the weather, can do a lot to counter the feelings of isolation our modern lifestyle all too often engenders.

Another benefit of making friends during your workout is that they provide motivation. When you are part of a team, you have an additional reason to show up for practice and games – you don't want to let everyone else down. Friendships can easily develop, and teammates often look out for each other. These strong bonds are good for your physical and emotional health.

So, as part of your campaign to be better organized and more productive at work, you need to look closely at how you manage your time outside the office. Make sure you get enough sleep, and make time for exercise, to boost your brainpower and increase your energy levels. As a bonus, you'll be keeping your heart healthy too, so you can hopefully look forward to a long and active retirement when you finally quit working.

Habit 13: Eat energy-giving foods!

'You are what you eat,' or so the saying goes, and you'd be amazed at how much the food you eat influences how you think, how you feel, and how it impacts on your overall health. When you're a busy person with lots to do every day, it's easy to take the easy option and eat out a lot. The problem with this is that usually eating out does not guarantee healthy food in the right quantities to maintain a healthy weight. The same goes for microwave convenience meals. These are usually pretty bad for you, because they are heavily processed, with added fats and sugars to make them look nicer and stay fresh for longer.

What you want is food that will actually nourish and fuel your energy and productivity. What foods might this be then? It's quite simple, actually – just eat natural. We could go into a whole discussion on different diets and their benefits, but for the sake of brevity here, I think the main focus for any diet you follow should be this: Focus on eating foods that naturally grow from the earth, trees, plants and farms. Try to eat as few processed foods as possible. Things like leafy greens, vegetables, fruits, nuts, and naturally raised meats will give you much more energy and sustenance than just eating greasy hamburgers, burritos, and sandwiches every day.

Healthy Eating Means Being In Balance

Another point worth remembering is that when you eat natural green foods, they help your body to be more "alkaline". Basically, there are two states your body can sway towards: alkaline and acidic. Research shows that when your body is in a more acidic state, this gives the opportunity for disease and illness to flourish. "Acidic" foods would be things like sugar, beer, beef and bread. The bottom line is that when you're eating foods that promote a more alkaline state, your immune system is stronger, you have more energy, and overall feel really, great. Just go Google "alkaline/acidic food chart" and you'll see what foods you should be eating.

If you make it a point to eat natural, alkaline-promoting foods, you will feel WAY more energetic when because you are eating healthily. It's a night and day difference. It gives you the energy and productivity to live an organized and productive day, every day.

The Mediterranean Diet

Just about the healthiest diet in the world is the Mediterranean Diet. That's something of a misnomer, because it's not actually a diet, it's a healthy eating plan followed by the people living in the area around the Mediterranean Sea. It's high on fruit, vegetables, fish, whole grains, pulses, dairy and lean poultry, and low on saturated fats, sugars and processed foods. Eat seasonal foods, because not only are they cheaper, they are also higher in natural nutrients.

The Mediterranean Diet is mostly alkaline, and it's high in antioxidants and Omega-3 fatty acids. That means it's heart healthy, and boosts your immune system, which will help you to stay fit and fight off infections. And because fish figures high on the list of regular foods, your brain gets nourished as well as your body.

How Eating Healthy Can Make You More Productive

Food provides us with much needed energy. We've talked already about how breakfast is a vitally important start to your day. Giving yourself a nutrient-rich beginning to the work day means you'll be able to think clearly and act in your own best interests at least through the early morning hours.

But what happens when the boost you've gotten from your healthy breakfast begins to wear off? Depending on your metabolism, you may start to feel sluggish an hour or two after you've arrived in the office – long before it's even close to lunchtime!

This is where strategic snacking can be your best friend. Stock your desk drawer or locker with energy-rich, healthy non-perishable snacks, such as nuts, dried fruits like raisins, or granola bars. You want to choose things that can be eaten discretely, without making a mess. Eat them during your mid-morning lull in energy; you may want another snack in the middle of the afternoon, when the energy pattern repeats itself.

Healthy snacks don't necessarily produce the immediate boost in energy and mood that come with high-sugar, high-fat treats like candy bars and donuts. On the other hand, the healthy snacks don't come with the excessively high amount of calories – and the energy healthy snacks do provide tends to be steadier and longer lasting than that sugary treats provides. Best of all, there's no 'sugar crash' to dread after eating a healthy snack!

Beware the break room donuts!

Sharing food is a very important part of our culture. Some workplaces have a tradition of bringing in baked goodies and other treats for everyone to enjoy. These foods are often very delicious, but they're a sure way to sabotage your plans for healthier eating.

One of the best things you can do is figure out a strategy to gracefully decline the break room donuts. Letting people know you're eating healthier can work, but it can also trigger competitive feelings among co-workers. Sometimes the best strategy is to smile and say 'Not today!' without any further explanation. Soothe over potential hurt feelings by saying "Oh, that looks delicious" about obviously home-baked treats. People put a lot of effort into making goodies and they want to know they're appreciated – even if you aren't eating them.

Have a Get Healthy Buddy

Working with someone is often easier than going it alone. This is especially true when it comes to getting healthy. If you have a like minded colleague, having healthy lunches and even going for walks or other fitness activities together can help you both get closer to achieving your goals.

Some workplaces actively promote wellness. If your employer offers a gym, fitness classes, nutrition counseling, or other health-related benefits, why not take advantage of them? Many of these services are quite expensive when you have to purchase them on your own. Use every resource you can to improve your life: it's a smart way to streamline your path to success.

Health Continues Past Quitting Time

As has been mentioned before, being more organized and productive extends beyond office hours. Take a close look at your diet, and make sure it is not holding you back from achieving all you are capable of. Some foods – particularly refined carbohydrates such as cakes, cookies and fast foods – actually drain your energy levels and make you sluggish and unresponsive at work. By fixing your diet, you are well on the way to creating the perfect recipe for success!

Habit 14: Plan ahead for meals

Following on from the previous section, if you're going to make it a point to eat healthy for better energy and productivity in your day, then you might also need to plan ahead for your meals. Depending on how busy you are throughout your days, you might not have time to make your own food on lunch break. Or maybe you get home really late and don't have time to cook a wholesome dinner.

Meal Prepping

If you're really pressed for time, I'd highly recommend you do what people are calling "meal prepping". This is where you think ahead for the next few days or week and figure out what you're going to eat, and then prepare the meals for those days as much as you need: be it breakfast, lunch, dinner or just one of those. You can make everything all in one batch on Sunday for example, then just store it in Tupperware containers in the fridge or freezer until needed.

If you don't already have one, invest in a crock pot. Then you can set a nourishing meal to cook slowly while you're at work. As a bonus, it will save on electricity and washing up, and you can use cheaper cuts of meat and poultry due to the extended cooking times. You should also consider investing in a halogen oven. It cooks up to 20% faster, and uses up to 75% less fuel too.

Food Delivery Services

One way to save yourself a lot of time, headache and hassle is to let go of the idea that you need to shop for and cook all of your meals yourself. Advances in technology have resulted in many new food delivery services which can bring prepared meals, frozen meals, and even fresh ingredients and instructions so you can cook your own meal directly to your door.

The cost of having food delivered tends to be slightly more expensive at first glance. But don't let sticker shock turn you off to this idea. Once you factor in the cost of your time and effort, having someone else do the meal prep can actually be a very cost effective option.

Many food delivery services have features to make your life easier. Explore the options available to you, such as auto-delivery, where food items can be brought to your home on a regularly recurring date, or online ordering, where you can select a week or even a month's worth of meals to be brought to you in advance.

Meal Sharing Plans

Another way to cut down on the amount of time you spend preparing meals is to plan regular get togethers with your friends. Maintaining a strong network of social relationships is important, and you can certainly talk to your best buddies over a meal at your favorite café.

Networking events often feature a light dinner or at least snacks. While I'm generally against multi-tasking in most forms, opportunities to combine the necessary task of eating with advancing your career are a treasure indeed. Just beware of the famous businessman's 3-martini lunch – they're generally not great for your waistline or professional development.

The Emergency Cupboard

Sometimes, the best plans in the world don't actually work out. You may find yourself at the end of an absolutely exhausting day with no food in the fridge, no delivery scheduled, no friends to meet up with, and a hunger that knows no bounds.

This is when the emergency cupboard becomes your best friend. Every household should maintain a cupboard that contains easy-to-prepare comfort foods, such as canned soup, microwavable entrees, or even pudding cups. While it's nice if these things are healthy, when you're short on time and energy, it's even more important that they're readily available, require next to no effort to prepare, and taste good.

Stock up your emergency cupboard on a day when you're feeling very productive and organized. Then shut the door and forget about it. Go about your plans for healthy eating by whichever method makes the most sense for you. The emergency cupboard will be there, waiting. When the day comes when terrible weather, ill health, or just an excessively long day means you can't even contemplate dealing with dinner, go to the emergency cupboard and enjoy the simple meals you've stored up there. It's a time saver you'll appreciate when you really need it.

These measures can free up your time immensely during the week, and cut back on the stress of trying to eat healthily while keeping up with a crazy schedule. Try it out and see how you get on. Remember, you are what you eat!

Habit 15: Give yourself time to recharge

This also might seem obvious, but many people are so go-go-go that they forget to stop, take a breather, and recharge their energy by relaxing. This is a good way to reward and encourage yourself after all your hard work. It's also a great way to unwind, clear your mind and get ready to take on future challenges. Figure out what makes you feel refreshed and recharged, and make it a habit to periodically do that. It could be going to the spa and getting a massage, taking a day to do nothing but relax with a good book, going out with friends, or anything else like that.

The important point is to just get out and have some fun, and unwind. Better yet, stay away from technology for a few hours. Leave your phone and your tablet at home, or just switch them off for a few hours. Facebook will still be there when you power up again!

Relationships matter

Remember not to neglect your family and close friends because of your busy schedule. Just because you're being productive doesn't mean you should neglect the people in your life that matter to you! Make sure you are giving your loved ones the attention and love they need and deserve from you. Whether it's your boyfriend, girlfriend, spouse, parents, kids, or best friends – don't forget about them and be sure to make time for them. Spending time with loved ones has a recharging effect in itself as well, and it will certainly reduce your stress levels.

Take a Humor Break

One of the best ways to recharge your batteries, boost your energy levels, and feel good about the life you're living is to laugh. Researchers have found that the act of laughing actually creates biomechanical changes in our bodies: blood pressure comes down, stress levels decrease, and the endorphins that control our mood start to skew in a positive direction when we enjoy humor.

Here's one time I will tell you to turn to social media. Look for funny Facebook pages or other online imagery that makes you laugh out loud. Everyone's sense of humor is different – look for the type of material that you find absolutely hysterical. YouTube is a great source of funny videos, while Netflix, Amazon Prime and other video streaming services have plenty of comedy.

Try to spend at least 15 minutes laughing. Laughter is a particularly vital tool when everything in your life has been going badly. Finding something amusing can distract you from the things that have been stressing you out. For that brief period of time, you're just focused on enjoying yourself. It's a smart way to feel better fast.

Feed Your Mind

Another way to recharge your batteries is to spend some time pursuing an intellectual or creative interest that has absolutely nothing to do with your job. It may seem counterintuitive, but it turns out that many of the world's top performers – entrepreneurs, scientists, physicians, and the like – all have hobbies that demand a lot of their energy and attention. The time they spend playing the violin or researching medieval castles or whatever captures their fancy actually makes them better at what they do professionally. Try it for yourself – one weekend afternoon should be enough to convince you of the value of outside interests.

By making time for yourself to recharge and time for others, you'll ensure that you don't burn out and that you can start each new day with the organization, productivity, and focus that you need to keep going. Taking a complete break from the work environment to do something you enjoy can actually make you more alert, productive and creative when you get back to business, so don't pass up on the chance to do something for you, rather than your boss or your business.

All work and no play makes Jack a dull boy, and Jill a dull girl, so don't let that happen to you. Managing your time efficiently means making time to unwind as well, so make sure you factor in some 'you' time, however hectic your schedule may be.

Habit 16: Keep your email under control!

Another often overlooked issue that affects your productivity is how often you spend checking, reading and responding to emails. Email has become an integral part life in the 21ˢᵗ century, but just like social media, it has the alarming potential to become a time consumer and a productivity killer as well. Given that almost everybody has a smartphone nowadays, email is even more "in your face" 24/7. Whenever you get a new email – your phone beeps, you look at it, swipe it open, and read whatever it's about. And this happens many times throughout the day.

This becomes problematic when it happens to the point of distracting you from whatever things you're trying to get done for the day. It may seem subtle, but if your phone goes off and you read 5 different emails and reply to them while trying to finish a task, it's quite possible you just wasted 30 minutes of your day right there. So to remedy this, you need to allocate a set time in the day where you review emails and that's it. Preferably this should be at the END of your day after you've accomplished all the important stuff. You can spend 30 minutes, 1 hour, or however long you need at the end of the day to read and reply to all of your emails. Of course, if you need to use email for work then that's an exception – just make sure your work emails are separated from your personal emails so that you don't get distracted while working!

Another thing to mention is that you can set up rules or "filters" in your email account to route different emails to different folders automatically. This will help you avoid inbox clutter so that when you sit down to sift through your emails, you only see the emails from important senders first (the ones you designate). All the other non-important emails can automatically go to folders where you can read them at a later time at your leisure. To learn more how to do this, just Google "email clutter best practices" or something similar.

If you are willing, you to do so, you can cut down on the amount of time you spend checking emails during the day. As an exercise, make a note of how many times you open your phone to check your emails during the day. You'll be both astounded and horrified! This should provide you with the motivation you need to get your emails under control and organize your day more productively.

Take time away from texting too!

Email can eat up hours of your day, but text messaging is almost as bad. If you're a Millennial or younger, texting may have supplanted email as your primary form of communication.

Because texts are short, they seem like they shouldn't be very time consuming. However, you can lose a good chunk of your day a few seconds at a time instead of in the many-minute blocks emails require. Be mindful about your texting habits: if you're spending more than a few minutes a day sending emoji-rich messages to anyone, you're wasting time!

Apps like Snapchat and Kik are increasingly important communications channels. Once the exclusive avenue of teenagers, now these apps are used by major brands. If you're using these apps, be mindful of how they're impacting your daily routine. Brief interactions can add up to a lot of time spent chatting!

It is a good idea to turn off your smartphone an hour before you go to bed. This allows your mind to prepare for a restful night's sleep. Another thing to consider is your phone's notifications. If your phone chimes, beeps, or vibrates every time you get a new text or app message, you're going to get distracted from other tasks you're trying to accomplish. Realistically, no one is going to turn off all of their notifications all of the time. But give yourself a block of time, preferably daily, where you're free from the digital dinging tether of smartphone notifications. It's a break for your psyche that will help boost your productivity.

Habit 17: Keep your home clutter-free

Last on the list of awesome productivity and organization hacks is - keep your home clutter-free! The reason this is important and worthy of inclusion on this list is because outside of being productive and working, you need a place where your mind and your body can relax.

Coming home to a house full of clutter and messes will NOT help ease your mind after a long day of being busy. This can affect your mood when you get home, add more stress, and even cause you to not sleep as well at night. These are all things that affect your productivity for the next day, so that's why it's so important. As has been mentioned several times in this book, being more organized and productive extends beyond the boundaries of the work place – it's a total way of life.

Cleanliness Saves You Time, Money and Stress

Developing the habit of a keeping your home tidy comes with three major benefits. The first is that you'll save a lot of time. If you've ever misplaced an important paper or your car keys, you know it can take forever to find them again. The hour you spend searching for the misplaced paper is an hour that could have been used in a much more productive fashion. When things are where you expect them to be consistently, you save time every single day.

The second benefit of keeping a tidy home is the fact you'll save money. It is not at all uncommon for people to purchase multiple copies of an item because they'd lost or misplaced the original. If you know exactly where your stapler is, for example, the odds are pretty good you won't purchase another stapler. But if you aren't even sure where to begin looking for your stapler, and you don't have time to search through a messy house for it, spending $10 to get another one seems like a sensible idea. But all of those small repeat purchases add up: eliminate those and save the money for something more fun, like a vacation.

Finally, keeping your house tidy will save you stress and heartache. We've talked about losing relatively trivial things, but what happens if you lose the only copy of vital paperwork or a truly sentimental, irreplaceable object? The emotional upheaval can be tremendous: combined with the fear of consequences of losing the object in question comes painful feelings of guilt and inadequacy. Nobody wants that! It's much easier to keep your home organized in the first place.

Less Clutter = More Happiness

As much as you find it comfortable fiddling with paperwork in bed or leaving dinner plates in the living room, it's best to put things back where they belong. Simply put, clutter-free surroundings result in a clutter-free mind. A clutter-free mind results in a more organized, productive, and successful you.

And really, don't use the excuse of "I'm too tired to clean." All you need to do is just power it out in 15 minutes before bed and clean up the biggest areas that need it, the areas that affect your state of relaxation the most. Use the 80/20 rule, remember? That's not saying you have to keep your house perfectly clean in all corners, but just keep it tidy enough to put things back in their place every night so that it doesn't get out of control!

If you really find it difficult to keep your home clean, tidy and clutter-free, why not use one of your productivity rewards to employ a cleaner, even if it's only one or two days a week?

Think of it as an investment in your success, and an exercise in delegation, because if you can remove that stress from your life, you can free that time to use for increased productivity at work or recharging time at home. Don't just dismiss it as an unnecessary extravagance – if it helps you to organize your time better and be more productive, it's worth every penny!

Conclusion

Hopefully this book will help you to come up with better ways to organize your day and give you more insight on how valuable it is to be organized and clutter-free in your life! The bonus is that better organization means better productivity, both at work and at home. If you manage your time more effectively, you'll have more leisure time too, which means you'll be happier and more relaxed, both at home and at work. And that means less stress all around.

As a next step, take action to implement the things you learned in this book. Start with the first few habits mentioned, which may be a bit more difficult to get a grasp on, and work forward from there. Tackle any necessary lifestyle changes once you are comfortable with the productivity hacks, rather than trying to implement everything at once. That will just get confusing.

Check back regularly to be certain you are doing what you need to do to organize your day better and become more productive. And read more extensively on the techniques you've been introduced to in this book. Review and readjust all the time. If a strategy is working, try to take it further; if it's not, try something else.

Remember to reward yourself even for the little wins in your life - you deserve it, and rewards will spur you on to even greater efforts and even more success!

Don't forget to turn the page to get my FREE BONUS GIFT offer just for you!

Here's your exclusive FREE BONUS!

Want to SAVE money on Kindle books, READ more, and WIN Amazon gift cards (and other prizes)?

If so, today's your lucky day! I'm able to give you FREE lifetime membership to my publisher's book club.

Here are the awesome things you get when you join the Epic Kindle Deals Book Club:

- FREE and 99c nonfiction books every week on health, diets, cooking, fitness, self-help, productivity and more!
- SAVE money on Kindle books (Never get any books over 99c!)
- WIN Amazon gift cards and other Amazon prizes in monthly giveaways!

This exclusive offer won't last forever, so **click below** to claim your spot and join now.

ENTER THIS LINK TO CLAIM YOUR SPOT: http://bit.ly/1PRXxhC

BONUS CHAPTERS

I want to share some FREE chapters with you, from my other time management and productivity books. I think you might like them as well!

Chapter from *"Time Management: To-Do List Strategies to Become a Productivity Master"*:

When you get up in the morning, no doubt you look at your do-it lists. You do need to put time aside for mundane tasks such as email and telephone calls, but the first thing that you need to decide upon each morning is what tasks on your do-it list are the top jobs for the day. That gives you a direction in which to work that day and allows you the luxury of seeing how to fit those jobs in with other criteria that may be imposed upon you. How fast you can access the information that you need in order to identify your top jobs for the day depends upon the **type of app that you choose**. Some find that simple to-do apps make this a lot easier. Some are simply set up a little bit like a grocery list, others are more complex. I personally find the simpler ones to be useful, but it depends on how complex your tasks and projects are. Since this book is targeted towards to-do list beginners, I'd recommend you start out with one of the apps mentioned below. They can easily integrate with your smartphone, computer, and tablet.

An app such as **Todoist** is ideal because it allows you to see all of the tasks that you have programmed for the day on one screen and from there to schedule a breakdown of the job and you can also use the app to share with others, which means that you can keep your team informed of what needs to be done. If you are using this app, you will find that it has the capability to set due dates (it's always better to set these a day in advance, so that you know exactly where you are). Your tasks on an app such as this should be prioritized so that you can see instantly which jobs are the vital ones for the day, while the others are lower priority.

Todoist can be broken down into 3 main sections: Filters, Labels and Projects. Each of these has important roles in managing your to-do lists. Projects can be organized in a hierarchal manner up to three levels. For example, classify my tasks as Personal, Family and Work. I'm a bit more particular or strict about work since it's what provides food on the table and roof over our heads, though I'm not particularly lax with the other two.

One of the keys to effectively managing to-do lists is making tasks actionable and simple. For example, instead of putting in "sell my fixie bike", I can put there the different actionable steps needed to actually complete it like "take picture of bike" and "post it online". Because it's much more actionable and specific, I'm less likely to put it off and more likely to act on it quickly.

For every task that needs multiple action steps, I create a project under the relevant category. In the fixie bike example earlier, I create the project under the Personal category, which is very useful when I conduct weekly reviews of my to-do lists because over time, some projects become less relevant. As such, I can easily remove all tasks that have anything to do with such projects.

I use different colors to make each project visibly distinct and easier to track. I can, for example, use light blue for work projects, gray for personal ones and dark blue for family-related ones.

Labels can provide a lot of help in terms of accomplishing tasks in our to-do lists. Personally, I use 3 label types, also with corresponding colors: today (blue), time-based (gray) and items in waiting (green). Items in the today list obviously mean I have to get them done within the day. Items labeled as time-based are those that have deadlines beyond today and items in waiting are those that require other peoples' actions before I can work on them.

You can personalize your own labels. For example, you can use "Church", "Extra-Curriculars" and "Community" as labels, among others. It's up to you. Whatever helps you organize your to-do items better, go for it...

Want to read more? Grab the book here on Amazon:
http://www.amazon.com/Time-Management--Do-Strategies-Productivity-ebook/dp/B0190D49SG/

Chapter from *"Time Management: Focus - Discover How to Get Amazing Focus, Concentration & Productivity That Gets You Results"*:

Motivation is something that may be lacking if people are throwing too much work at you, but you can use it to power up your approach. I always teach people that motivation is power and the motivation should come from inside you. There is nothing better than knowing you are fully in control and that's what motivates you each and every day, once you have learned to fire it up. It's a question of self-satisfaction more than anything else. You can also be  motivated by people that you admire and being in touch with positive people who share your desire to go forward in your life is a great idea. These are the kind of people who show, through their example, what it is to achieve.

Focus

The part that focus plays in your work life is vital. If you take up the system that I previously suggested, your concentration areas are defined areas when you know that you will have no interruptions and these are times when the difficult work is handled. The motivation with the bulk work is the satisfaction of seeing it all done and going home in the evening knowing that everything on your desk was dealt with. That's a great feeling because it allows you to enjoy your down time with your family. There is a great work/home life balance that you need to achieve. If you let your home life eat into your work life, you lose motivation quickly and if work life imposes too much on your family time, then your family time becomes less satisfactory. Thus, if you have done everything that you were supposed to have done, you can go home and relax and that relaxation really is necessary for your wellbeing.

Enjoying the two elements of your life

If you want to have a lot of energy the next day at work, you need to have time with your family the night before and you also need to achieve a good night's sleep. That way, you wake up with the motivation that follows you through the rest of the day. If your private time and your work time are overlapping, you need to do something to make sure that they are separate entities, even if that means adjusting your work life to suit your home life or vice versa. This slots time periods into your life where your concentration isn't pulled back and forth and you are able to give whatever you have to whatever it is that you are doing. That in itself motivates.

Inspiration

Perhaps you are lacking in inspiration after you have done the hard work of the morning, but you can regain this. If you go somewhere away from the work place at lunchtime and sit in an inspirational area, this can rejuvenate your enthusiasm. For example, in a large city, there are ample parks where you can just cut yourself off from the workplace. You may even find that taking up meditation will help you with your energy levels as well. This is certainly food for thought.

Splitting work into manageable packages

If you are overwhelmed by what you have to do, even when you have prioritized the urgent work or the work that will take the most concentration, then you need to follow this guide because it helps motivation levels to rise. Look at the whole job. It's huge and it's frightening and you are not sure that you can do it by the goal deadline. Now, split it into smaller and more manageable tasks and it becomes a lot easier. If you schedule the tasks so that the whole job finishes on the set deadline, you will find that you are much more motivated because you know that each small task is doable. You are not seeing a huge daunting task lying in front of you, but a split of that task into small jobs that you know you have the capability to finish. Concentrate on each element of the job and give yourself deadlines for finishing each section of that job. Work on one section at a time, only referring to others when you need to. It really can help you.

When given a payroll to run off on the computer, the vastness of the task was too much for Eleanor. However, when she split this into smaller tasks, she was able to excel at it. She took different groups of people who needed to be paid and made these into batch runs so that she could see the end of one batch and the beginning of another. That made more sense to her and she managed to finish all of the jobs that she had before time because of this organizational change. This motivated her more than looking at a huge task that seemed too much for one person. However, by splitting it, she managed to achieve much more than usual and was even able to have free time left at the end of the day. This achievement of a job really does motivate you for the next job and the next.

If you are really lacking in motivation, you need to adjust your job so that each part of it is manageable and achieve one part at a time, thus making the goal areas much more likely to be achieved. You can do it and this really will give you the motivation.

Want to read more? Grab the book here on Amazon: http://amzn.to/1S0VroN

Did you like this book?

If you liked this book (or if you didn't), I'd love to hear your feedback and if it helped you. I welcome all feedback and use it to make my books better, so please leave a review for the book on Amazon if you have 30 seconds here:
http://amzn.to/1WeRZmY

Questions? Concerns? Please email us at epicpublishingbooks[at]gmail.com.